The Call of the Small

Kimberly Davis

BARE COVE PRESS
Hingham, MA USA

Copyright © 2013 Kimberly Davis

All rights reserved. No part of this book may be used or reproduced in any manner without written permission of the author.

ISBN-10: 0983481059
ISBN-13: 9780983481058
Library of Congress Control Number: 2013919477
Bare Cove Press, Hingham, MA -cny(10/25/2013)

[Photo copyrights; Photo permissions]

For permissions and reprints, please contact:
Bare Cove Press, P.O. Box 699, Hingham, MA 02043.

The Call of the Small

**OR, HOW I STOPPED HATING TINY LAPDOGS
(AND GOT ONE OF MY OWN)**

Kimberly Davis

Bare Cove Press
Hingham, MA USA

For Steve and Daniel

AUTHOR'S NOTE

The events I have set down here are true, and I have tried to relate them as accurately as I could, given an imperfect memory and the elapse of ten years. That being said, I have changed the names and disguised the identities of the other families involved in order to protect their privacy. I should add that the children depicted in these pages will by now have grown into young adults, and so it seems the right time for this story to be told. I sincerely hope that those children—wherever they are—understand that nothing that happened was their fault. If at times I have sounded less than generous toward them in the recounting of this narrative, it has been only to record my own deficits of character and lack of empathy with as much clear-eyed veracity as I could muster. In rescuing Sadie, I certainly was no saint. I can only hope those young people know that they have my genuine good will, and that my warmest thoughts are with them as they proceed forward with their own adult lives and families. I am telling this story mainly to put into perspective all that occurred in my own mind, so that I may be the wiser for it.

Kimberly Davis, Fall 2012

PROLOGUE—JUNE 2002

"Go and get the dog," the children's father said.

I stood with him in the hot sun of an early June day and watched his kids race towards the house—a girl and a boy, aged 9 and 12. They were going to retrieve the tiny Maltese dog I had reluctantly come to take from them. Though the children were losing their dog to me, at least for the time being, they seemed at this moment anxious to find her and show her off to me—their prized possession—the small purebred lapdog that had been their mother's beloved and much pampered pet. They shoved against each other as they ran towards the big grey mansion, seeming suddenly much younger children, each jostling against the other sibling for position.

They disappeared into their home for a moment, and then reappeared, the boy carrying in his arms what could barely still be described as a dog—a shivering, rat-like creature, yellow on top and with an underside the reddish-brown color of mud. The children seemed unable to see their dog's condition, were strangely immune to the harrowing impression created by this emaciated, nearly hairless thing. It was as if they could only imagine her as she had once been, with her lovely white show-coat and pink bow perched jauntily atop her brow.

"Look!" the boy cried, "she can walk on my shoulders."

He boosted the tiny figure up on his shoulders and neck. The pathetic creature, mustering what strength she could, scrambled about on her skinny legs with their black overgrown toenails, her huge dark waif-eyes gazing back at us. It was as if she were desperately trying to entertain her assembled audience, a sad little clown with tearstained makeup.

"All right, that's enough," the children's father said at last. He plucked the dog briskly off his son's shoulders, plainly embarrassed. A harsh note entered his voice as he told the kids, "Say goodbye now and go back in the house."

What happened next happened very fast. Too fast. The father carried the dog over to my car, where it was parked in the driveway in front of the house, and tossed her in the backseat, leaving me free to climb back into the driver's seat myself. And then we were pulling out of the driveway, the wheels of the car spinning on fine white gravel, as the boy cried out and rained his fists down hard on the metal side of the car. It was a sharp knuckled sound, like hailstones hitting the car. I remember the father wrapping his arms around the boy's waist from the rear to pull him away from the car, and lifting his half-grown son into the air as easily as if he were made of cardboard. The girl, too, was protesting, and her cry rang out like a bell upon the still, warm June air.

Chapter 1

"I HATE SMALL DOGS"

The first thing you need to know is that I never meant to get involved with the impromptu rescue of a tiny lapdog. The fact is, I have always loathed miniature pet dogs.

I have noticed that most people tend to have some sort of stance towards these "teacup" pooches that you seem to see everywhere these days. Either they are *for them* or *against them*. There are the "converted" types who burst into crooning at the very sight of these little ambassadors for the dog world and begin uttering the kootchy-koo phrases generally reserved for babies. Then there are the small dog "haters" (as I have always been) who, upon seeing a tiny lapdog tucked under an arm, will form their mouths into a just-bit-into-an-onion pucker of distaste and will begin to utter vague obscenities.

The rest of humanity, the middle third as I think of them, tend not to be lukewarm about small dogs, but rather—like the undecided voters we see at election time—veer wildly between these two extremes. One moment you will hear "the undecided" complaining about how obnoxious these tiny excuses for a purse are, and *Must they really sit with us at dinner?*

And the next moment—this usually happens after a tiny dog has been plopped onto a lap at a dinner party—you will hear these same people saying, *Well, I don't usually like little dogs, but this one here is a real doll, an exception to the rule*, and *Lord, don't you just love her, kootchy-koo*, and off they go, lost to the charms of six wriggling pounds of adoration and a large pair of liquid eyes.

But, as I have said, and I must remind you, I was firmly and steadfastly planted for most of my life in the Hater Camp.

How did I get there?

As with most such religious beliefs, I was indoctrinated as a young child, before I could independently form my own opinions. I was inculcated in the Art of Small Dog Hating in my own childhood home. By my own mother, rest her soul.

I grew up the first twelve years of my life at the western edge of a small upstate New York town where my father—fresh off the dairy farm and having earned an engineering degree from a good college—had set up a construction company with one of his former professors. They were building commercial properties back then, mostly paper mills, around the northeastern United States. It was a time of growing prosperity for my family, and for most of the country, and my mother—despite having pretentions to joining the burgeoning women's movement—had the luxury of being a nineteen-sixties housewife.

I have to say, my mother was the best mother in the world. She was smart and theatrical, acting out the books she read to us, hauling us off to every intellectual pursuit available in that rustic backwater, hiking us up and down the mountains of the Adirondacks, and regularly scheduling family adventures out to see the rest of the world. (She was determined that my brother and I not be hampered by our rural upbringing.) Our home was the site of every play date in our neighborhood, and of every birthday party, baseball game, frog collecting adventure, and sledding expedition.

Still—despite her kindness, her intelligence and generosity—my mother did have one small prejudice. And I say "small" here advisedly, and with emphasis.

Like my father, my mother had grown up on a dairy farm, where dogs were dogs, meaning big dogs, and where everyone worked all the time. And she had a special loathing in her heart for the Pomeranian owned by our next-door neighbors. Her attitude toward this tiny neighbor dog seemed connected with the general uselessness of the animal. I don't recall her ever actually taking me aside and saying, *Look here, we don't DO small dogs in this house.* They are useless as working dogs; you can't eat them (as tempting as that prospect might be in some corners); and the only people who would have them are degenerate types who don't know any better and have pretensions to luxury. The message, though, was communicated.

Small dogs were, to my mother's mind, a good indicator of a certain sort of "nouveau riche" mentality growing in the United States. Tiny lapdogs were a symptom, a sign, a red flag marking vulgar suburbanites who had too little work to do, and too much time on their hands for things like watching television. (Actually, come to think of it, my mother had a similar prejudice against color TV's, and persisted resolutely in watching her fuzzy black and white set through the end of the nineteen-seventies, long after everyone else we knew had relented to color.)

What I think is interesting is that, not only was I indoctrinated in small dog despising from a young age, but my mother was already doing something you see over and over again in discussions of the merits of small dogs, which was filtering social and cultural commentary through the lens of people's dog-owning habits. This will become important for us later, particularly as we get into the growth of celebrity media culture in the United States, and how it has fed the rage for lapdogs.

The point I want to make here is that this is nothing new. As long ago as the late nineteen-sixties, I saw my own mother making assumptions about our neighbors based upon the kinds of dogs they owned. And the assumptions were—let us say—less than kind. But in fairness to my dear departed mother, I must add that the prejudices she communicated to me as a child were soon dwarfed by my own personal dislike for the prickly six-pounder next door, developed through my actual encounters with the little beast.

The neighbors who owned the Pomeranian were a French Canadian family whom we shall call the LeBlancs. The oldest son, Jeff LeBlanc, was my twin brother's best friend, and one of our regular neighborhood companions for baseball games and for playing around the yard. My brother Tim and I would go next door to "get Jeff" to come over to our house for whatever game or activity my mother had cooked up. I don't think we ever actually went *into* the LeBlanc house. Jeff's mother was also a stay-at-home mom, and at the cracking open of their front door one was instantly assaulted by a fog of cigarette smoke and the blare of a large color television set, both of which we had been let know at our home were unhealthy items. And so Tim and I would quickly retrieve Jeff and beat a hasty retreat back to our own yard. In the course of this mission to "get Jeff," however, we would also encounter the LeBlancs' two dogs.

One of the dogs was a medium sized and mustachioed terrier that belonged to Jeff himself. This dog followed Jeff everywhere, and was dubbed "Spotty," an appropriate name given that Spotty's long moustaches always appeared to have been freshly dipped in bright red spaghetti sauce. (Looking back, I suspect that the LeBlanc household was probably eating Spaghetti-O's for lunch every day—canned Spaghetti-O's were very popular back then—and Spotty was probably consuming the leftovers.) In any event, there was this Spotty dog, and then there was also the TERRIBLE POM, which appeared not to have a name. Or rather, you never had the time to learn its name, because the moment this teensy Teddy Bear-looking dog spied you, it immediately went on the offensive.

I have a very vivid childhood memory of this diminutive cinnamon-colored tyke as an all-out snapping, snarling blur behind the LeBlancs' door, and of Jeff and Spotty squeezing themselves out the aluminum storm while trying not to release this frightening, if miniscule, monster. In retrospect, it's a little hard to imagine that, even as a child, I was actually scared by this animal. The creature must have weighed all of six or seven pounds, and one good boot to the solar plexus would have sent it flying to the moon. Still, it was awful to see any house pet this angry, or this determined to kill you and rip out your lungs, even one this small. No, not *awful*, that's the wrong word. Appalling. Or horrifying. *Horrifying*. Yes, that's the word I'm searching for. I was *horrified* by this tiny canine menace. Honestly, it was like watching a horror movie on TV, such as *The Fly* or *The Blob*. An animal that was supposed to be a docile little lapdog had transformed itself into a grotesque and threatening freak and was doing its best to tear your throat to shreds.

Of course, this dog was too short to reach your throat, or, for that matter, even your knee. On those rare occasions when this army-of-one managed to escape its dented aluminum door, it went for the only thing that it could reach, which was straight for your ankles. And so, my other vivid memory of this tiny dog, besides seeing it raging shrilly behind the LeBlancs' door in a cloud of cigarette smoke, is of it dangling from my pants leg by its teeth as I tried to shake it off. I remember wondering vaguely whether it had rabies—since rabies was causing an epidemic among the skunks and raccoons in our town at the time. This little dog's face had a crooked possum-like snout and thick bristling fur that stood out straight from its body, which further confirmed its rabid-rodent effect. I also recall Jeff's overweight and soap-opera viewing mother, in her loose shapeless housedress, lumbering slowly out the door and bending to delicately unclamp the rabid rat from my leg, whereupon the Pom would settle calmly upon her corpulent arm, blowing upon its freshly manicured nails with an air of satisfaction at having accomplished its task.

Is it any wonder that I grew up hating little dogs?

My mother must have viewed this recurring drama from our own yard with a few self-righteous clucks of disapproval, and not a little amusement. Of course, she couldn't know how things would later turn out.

Prejudice. It is a powerful thing, and is not easily undone. My dislike of tiny lapdogs settled firmly into my brain, along with my distaste for cigarette smoke, loose house dresses on middle-aged women, and blaring soap operas. My mother's lessons had taken solid root. These prejudices hardened, calcified, and went unchallenged for many years, all through college and my young working life in large law firms in my twenties and early thirties. During this time, I met not a single lapdog to challenge the stereotype.

On those rare occasions when I did encounter tiny pet dogs, they seemed invariably to fly into the same sort of unprovoked attack as the Pom. And I began to form a stereotype, not just of the dogs themselves, but also of the well-dressed, high-maintenance, skeletally-thin women upon whom they tended to drape themselves. The lapdogs often wore clothing that matched the owner's, usually something featuring animal prints. These dogs were more of a fashion statement, really, genetically closer to designer handbags than actual living creatures. They were ornaments to be carried about by affluent, older, city-dwelling ladies, a commodity quite irrelevant to my own life and home, and I found them easy to dismiss.

Then something happened. Beginning in the late nineteen-nineties, suddenly these miniature dogs were everywhere: Chihuahuas, Maltese, Yorkies, Morkies, French Bulldogs. You remember this, right? The Internet age had arrived, bringing with it the attendant growth of celebrity media culture. And alongside this development, small lapdogs began appearing on the arms of starlets and prepubescent girls everywhere.

The little dogs seemed especially to come to the fore of public consciousness sometime around 2001 with the release of the movie *Legally Blonde*, which spoofed this trend by tucking a pink-clad Chihuahua named Bruiser under the arm of star Reese Witherspoon. The movie dumped gasoline on the fire, and sent trendsetters everywhere scurrying for their own tiny accessory-dogs, the most popular breeds back then being Maltese and Chihuahuas, the smaller and more handbagesque the better.

Then, around 2003, the American public got an eyeful of Paris Hilton cuddling her Chihauhua, Tinkerbell, on the set of the new reality series, *The Simple Life*, with Nicole Richie. Suddenly the viewing audience was watching nightly as Hilton hugged this miniscule creature, babied her, fed her, and dressed her in diminutive dog clothing, while Hilton and Richie cavorted through real life rural adventures, such as milking cows. The barn stalls and milking parlors of my youth were literally being invaded by tiny lapdogs.

It wasn't long before every starlet worth her salt was being photographed in the West Village or Santa Monica with a teensy pet dog clutched in her manicured hands. Lindsay Lohan had a Maltese named Chloe; Britney Spears a Chihuahua named Bit Bit. There are too many starlets and little dogs to list. Over the next five or six years the celebrity rage for the small dog burned unabated, the history glowingly and indelibly preserved, if you wish to see it, on *The Celebrity Dog Blog*, which dishes up the historical pictures year by year online.

The lapdog frenzy seemed to reach its rather desperate apex sometime around 2008 or 2009—perhaps not coincidentally about the same time as the housing crash hit. You knew the party was over when Jessica Simpson's Malti-poo, Daisy, a gift from her celebrity ex-husband Nick Lachey, was reportedly snatched from Simpson's L.A. backyard by a coyote, leading to an all-out manhunt (or should I say doghunt?) for the missing mite.

This drama, which played out daily in the tabloids and online, may or may not have been connected with efforts to revive the fortunes of a teen idol rapidly approaching her sell-by date. (Paris Hilton's Tinkerbell had similarly gone missing in 2004, apparently to hype the release of a book supposedly "authored" by the tiny Chihauhua.) Who knew if any of this stuff was true? Who even cared? In any event, dognapping became the story of the hour, and the disappearances of celebrity and non-celebrity lapdogs were covered by the media with the breathless urgency that had once attended the Lindbergh baby kidnapping.

I have to say that, at least at first, I was only dimly aware of this growing rage for tiny lapdogs. By the late nineteen-nineties, I was myself a stay-at-home mom in the suburbs south of Boston. I had dropped off the legal "fast track" when I'd had my son Daniel, and around the same time my mother got sick with lymphoma, a two-year battle she would eventually lose. I was nursing along a fledgling writing career on the back-burner while spending most of my days supervising the activities of a small child. As the McMansions sprouted around us, ever larger and larger, and the SUV's grew from Jeep Cherokees into Rolling Living Rooms, another presence began to make itself felt. Oddly, as everything else around us grew bigger and bigger (the houses, the cars), the dogs seemed quite visibly to shrink.

What could account for this phenomenon? I remember wondering about this at the time.

Had I missed something? Had the suburban degeneracy my mother worried about reached its logical conclusion?

The tiny dogs did seem symptomatic of some sort of excess in American culture—something having to do with conspicuous consumption and excess credit which later would find its proof in the form of the bursting housing bubble and the financial crisis.

In any event, at the time there was no missing it, not even for someone as oblivious and otherwise preoccupied as myself: The little dogs had arrived. And unbeknownst to me, one was headed in my direction, like a tiny force of nature, determined to change my mind.

Chapter 2

FALL 1999: HOW IT BEGAN

I first met Sadie the Maltese in 1999, three years before she would become an active presence in my life. She appeared as a tiny white puppy at our local school bus stop, on the arm of one of the other mothers. My son Daniel, at the time, was a first-grader at our local public school in North Marshfield, Massachusetts, a suburban community organized around a point on the North River near where it discharged into the blue Atlantic. In this partly-rural suburb on Boston's South Shore, "free-ranging" Labradors and Golden Retrievers were then the norm for dogs. In fact, when we moved into our house in the mid-nineties, I remember how the neighbors all joked that "every house on the street came with a yellow dog." They meant a BIG yellow dog. But not for long.

With all the McMansions springing up on what had formerly been a sleepy "Townie" point on the river, home to tradesmen and lobster boats, our area was rapidly being invaded by a more affluent set to which I'm sure many of our neighbors viewed my lawyer husband and myself as belonging—although our own home was an ancient waterfront cottage that threatened to sink like an old boat with every high tide.

This neighborhood very much reflected the changes in American society of the late-nineties to mid-aughts, when outer ring suburbs near large cities were becoming the situs of an outrageous and aspirational building boom. And so Daniel and I would find ourselves each morning walking down the road from our circle of ramshackle bungalows on the river to stand at a bus stop at the foot of a large hill upon which had been freshly constructed ten or twelve of these "McMansions."

I had never known anyone who lived in these faux mansion before, and I thought the houses very strangely styled. They were large boxy structures which seemed roughly based upon the design of a New England Colonial, but they would haphazardly sprout the dormer windows more often found on a Cape, or a farmer's porch from the Victorian Era, or perhaps Monticello looking columns. Regardless of their varied features, what distinguished these residences—and set them apart from the other homes in the neighborhood—was their great size. They utterly dwarfed the Capes, ranches and traditional colonials that had heretofore comprised the bulk of the New England housing stock.

Standing at the bus stop in the morning, I was also suddenly surrounded by a cluster of foiled-blondes who lived in these imposing structures, all of them appearing to my eye to be at least six feet tall, and all of whom drove enormous, exhaust-spewing SUVs. Although I had gone to an Ivy League college, I still carried with me the rural skepticism of an upstate New Yorker, and I remember feeling amazed, dubious and rather affronted by my first taste of this particular brand of suburban affluence, huge mansions, gleaming black or white SUV's, trophy wives.

Fall 1999: How It Began

Also, I have to say that I felt I had little in common with these upscale suburban moms. I was a bit older, having already had a professional career that spanned fifteen years and two major cities, and I remember feeling somewhat excluded by their group. I'm sure they viewed me as snobbish or weird or a little daft, since I found their usual chatter—which focused almost exclusively upon topics of home economics—to be rather mind-numbing, and I had trouble focusing on what they said. In fairness to them, though, I was also at that time in a constant state of distraction, being deeply immersed in an MFA program in creative writing at a Boston college. I was stumbling to the bus stop mornings in my pajamas after having been out at writing classes the night before, and I'm sure that I was shoving dirty hair out of my eyes and muttering to myself while clutching a cold cup of coffee with an air of rushed desperation.

I would usually exchange a few hellos with these other mothers as we saw our children off on the school bus, and then would fall silent while I listened to the bus stop chatter, which was mostly about where one could buy things cheaply. After awhile, hearing nothing of immediate consequence to my present concerns, I would make my way back down the road to our cottage to wrestle with some arcane point of writing craft while the others roared off in their Tahoes and Navigators, on their way to work or the gym or whatever.

On one particular morning, though, I remember that everyone was oohing and cooing over a tiny new Maltese puppy in the arms of one of the mothers. This woman was not a blonde, actually, but was a tall narrow dark-haired woman, named Calista Piero. Calista had large pale blue-green eyes, beautiful tanned skin, and the unerring fashion sense that some women seem to possess, her hair constantly shifting through the latest trendy hairstyles. She worked part-time as a real estate agent, and was married to the developer who had built several of the McMansions on the hill. (As a result, she and her family lived in one of the largest of these ostentatious homes.) She had two school-age kids at the bus stop, an older boy and a little girl of six or seven for whom the Maltese presumably had been purchased—though the dog appeared from casual inspection to belong mainly to Calista.

As the bus pulled away that morning, I remember how Sadie—who was then still a puppy and probably weighed all of three pounds—the size of a guinea pig or a Yukon Gold potato—lay draped demurely across Calista's arm while the other mothers petted and admired her. The tiny dog was sparklingly white in her long flaxen coat, and had the obligatory pink bow perched atop her rounded forehead to hold the hair out of her eyes. Her bright black shoe button eyes and nose explored curiously and happily the hands that reached out to touch her, and she occasionally put out a paw to bat at them like a kitten, or uttered a sharp little bark which could have been mistaken for the tweet of a goldfinch.

I was not completely immune to the charms of this diminutive curiosity. I had never seen a dog even remotely this small—she truly could fit into a teacup—or one so playfully vivacious. And so I waited my turn, and then put out my own hand. Sadie's curly tail, which she held gaily up over her back, waived merrily, and I recall the warm, brief slide of her tongue across my proffered fingers. The whole scene had the air of a small playful princess holding court from her accustomed divan. I wondered momentarily if I'd had this whole lapdog thing all wrong. My sudden shift in sentiments is difficult to account for today, but there was a rush of ardor for tiny dogs in the air back then, in 1999, and it was a trend that the fashionable Calista had swiftly picked up on. And, like any good fashion trend, this fervor had managed to communicate itself to even the most style-clueless person, like me.

Sadly, my change of heart was not to last.

A day or two later I brought my own dog to the bus stop—I, too, had a puppy at home back then, though mine was much larger—a half-grown rough collie, named Willow. Willow was a sweet sociable Lassie-dog, and absolutely adored children, and he hated being left behind while we walked to the bus stop in the morning. So I often allowed him out the door with Dan and me, snapping a leash on him so that he wouldn't run in front of the bus.

On this particular morning, I remember that we were early to the bus stop, and Dan ran off with a shout to play with the other children. I clicked Willow off his leash so that he, too, could run around with the kids, but instead—like me—he drifted over to say hello to Sadie, who was again resting on Calista's arm.

I recall that Willow put up his long collie nose to sniff at what presumably registered in his olfactory system as "another dog," and then, abruptly, everything changed. Suddenly and without warning, Sadie launched herself at my adolescent collie with a shrill snarl that sounded like a little scream. She thrashed about growling and snapping, and threatened to fall to the ground—though Calista managed to catch and restrain her.

Poor Willow. He was always a bit on the meek side as a puppy, and he beat a terrified retreat from this high-pitched and unprovoked attack from above, nearly managing to dart under the wheels of the approaching bus. I swiftly caught him, and dragged him out of the way, and then turned back to Calista, my eyes wide with alarm.

Calista's eyes were equally wide, and accusatory (her dog was still growling and squealing), and she nearly shouted at me—as if Willow or I had done something terribly wrong, "She's afraid of big dogs!"

Afraid?! I remember thinking. *Afraid??*

For the record, Sadie didn't look the least bit afraid. Willow was the one who looked afraid. Sadie looked like she was having a ball, launching a surprise attack upon a much larger dog and frightening the bejesus out of him. And now, after having had my poor puppy attacked in this way, this was all somehow supposed to be *my fault?*

One of the alpha blondes stepped between Calista and me, and announced—in a tone designed to avert further discussion—that if the two dogs couldn't get along then we would simply have to leave them both at home when we came to the bus stop.

Both? I thought. *Now, wait a minute . . . .*

Knowing what I do now about Sadie, I wonder if she hadn't already attacked some of the other bigger dogs in the neighborhood, and whether this incident didn't simply provide an opportunity for the other mothers to ban her from the bus stop before one of their big yellow dogs snapped her in two, or ate her. At the time, though, I didn't appreciate this, and I was furious that my own puppy, who loved coming to the bus stop, was now apparently being banished by this bossy blonde when he had done absolutely nothing wrong, and was in fact the injured party. I probably opened my mouth in feeble protest, but I was already an outcast among this group, while Calista was an esteemed member of the bus stop crowd, and I could see there was no point in trying to argue.

I remember huffing back from the bus stop that morning muttering under my breath. *Afraid, huh? Afraid, my eye!*

Poor Willow. Always the sweet, sensitive fellow, he took half the morning to recover from Sadie's Kamikazee attack. He kept looking up nervously, as if expecting more flying Maltese dogs to suddenly dive-bomb him from the air. The poor guy, I thought. He still didn't know what had hit him.

The incident certainly had done nothing to improve my opinion of these teensy lapdogs. My mother was right, I thought. I would NEVER have one of those little pocket monsters in my home.

Calista and I later made further efforts to introduce our two dogs—away from the bus stop, and with Sadie on the ground and not attacking Willow from above. But the moment Calista would let go of Sadie, the little Maltese would fly at my young collie, snapping and snarling. At last we agreed that the bossy blonde had indeed been right. The only solution was to leave the two dogs at home.

I began to wonder if this attacking thing was congenital with small dogs. Were they all like this? And if so, why?

We didn't see much of the belligerent half-pint Sadie after that, except for occasionally catching glimpses of her elfin face poking out the tinted windows of Calista's huge black SUV as they roared past us on the main road from the point while Willow and I were out walking.

At the end of the school year, my husband and I transferred Daniel to a private Montessori school in Hingham, MA, another town north of us. The Marshfield public schools were not proving a good fit for my cerebral son. And so we no longer stood at the bus stop in the mornings. I pretty well lost touch with the other mothers—though we still lived in the same neighborhood and I sometimes still ran into them.

I would occasionally see one of the bus stop crowd while I was out walking Willow, or when I was outside gardening in the yard. At those moments I would get an update on the neighborhood news. A couple of years went by in this fashion, and I more or less forgot about Sadie the wee terror.

Chapter 3

GUILT

As time passed, the one bus stop mom whom I ran into the most was a tall blonde nurse named Peggy Marsten. This was because Peggy lived the closest to us, just a couple of houses away. And, like me, Peggy kept odd hours—in my case because I was finishing grad school, and in her case because she was spending four nights a week helping deliver babies at a large Boston hospital so she could be home with her kids after school. As a result we were both around the neighborhood in the afternoons, and we sometimes had the chance to talk.

Peggy turned out to be a lovely person, very kind and sweet, and when I ran into her we would spend a few moments catching up. I wouldn't go so far as to call us good friends, but she did keep me apprised of what was happening around the point. It turned out that her daughter, Alexandra, was close pals with Calista's daughter, Tessa, so over time I began to get occasional snapshots of what was going on with Calista's life.

The story was far different from anything I could have imagined based upon our previous encounters. For one thing, Calista was battling ovarian cancer. The constantly shifting hairstyles I had previously attributed to her fashion sense were actually a series of wigs she had been wearing to hide her hair loss from chemotherapy.

I don't know how I missed this, having just been through the same thing with my own mother. Perhaps I wanted to miss it, having just been through the same thing with my mother. And Calista truly was very fashion forward. (If capes were in vogue, she could be counted on to appear at the bus stop in a cape. If cropped pants were in, you could be sure she'd be sporting a pair of cropped pants.) So it wasn't out of the question that she might change her hairstyles frequently.

At any rate, sometime after I heard this dreadful news from Peggy, one of the other bus stop mothers told me that Calista's husband, the developer, had left her. They were furious at him—the bus stop moms—for walking out on Calista when she had cancer. I remember Peggy referring to this fellow as "abusive" and "bipolar," and speaking about him with a level of vitriol in her voice that wasn't like her. I didn't know what to make of this, since I didn't know the man in question. Still, it seemed as if something bad had to have happened to make someone as sweet as Peggy so angry and nasty. I remember her telling me that Calista's husband had wasted no time in getting himself a new girlfriend. It was just unbelievable, she said, shuddering. Just beyond belief.

I felt terrible for Calista and her two kids—for little Tessa Piero and her older brother Robbie. I guess I wasn't altogether surprised, though, that Calista's husband had taken off on her. I remembered how, after my own mother was diagnosed with cancer, many of our family and friends had disappeared. Cancer is so scary that the mere mention of it is enough to make many people flee.

The bus stop moms, though, they didn't run away. They pitched in, helped out with the kids, cleaned Calista's house. I don't know if it was because Peggy was a nurse, or what, but that group of mothers seemed to know almost instinctively what to do.

Or so I gather.

As I've said, I was no longer in daily contact with the bus stop moms, and I only heard about most of this drama after the fact. During this period I was finishing my thesis for my MFA, which involved producing an entire draft of a novel in short order. I was also constantly driving my son back and forth between Marshfield and his new school and friends in Hingham. We were already considering a move further up the South Shore, to Hingham for the public school system—private school was getting expensive—and we were starting to look for a house up there. And, in the midst of all of this, my husband was in the process of leaving the large Boston law firm where he'd been working, and was setting up his own practice down on the South Shore. So we were rarely around, and even when we were, my attention was far away from what was happening in our little seaside community. I had no idea that Calista's situation was becoming dire. I had actually seen her out walking a few times, and except for her lack of hair, which she now concealed under scarves and hats, she seemed to be doing pretty well. She always seemed to be exercising.

I remember, though, that after a period of a year or two—it was now a cold blustery day in January or February of 2002—I was out walking Willow down the main road to the point, when a white minivan pulled up beside us, and the window rolled down. It was Peggy, the nurse.

"Did you hear about Calista?" she said. Her voice was husky.

We had just been away somewhere warm. I hadn't heard anything. "What about her?" I asked.

"She passed away last week."

Peggy told me how she and the other bus stop moms had been there with Calista at the end, and how fast she'd gone downhill.

"And the kids?" I asked.

Peggy told me that Bob Piero, Calista's ex-husband, had moved back into their house on the hill during the final weeks of Calista's life in order to care for the kids, now nine and twelve. He was still living with them up there in the Pieros' mansion, but they were planning to move away as soon as possible, to a new place. Calista's death was still too fresh for everyone, and they needed to get out of that house.

I was stunned. I had been so out of touch, as I have said, that it all seemed very sudden and tragic. Shocking. Horrible.

I also think that I felt a strong stab of survivor guilt that I didn't then connect with having recently lost my own mother. I had known that Calista was sick, I thought, but I hadn't reached out to her. Sure, I hadn't realized how serious her condition was, but that now seemed like a feeble excuse. I felt I should have done something more. I had also grossly under-estimated the bus stop mothers. I had regarded them as shallow and vapid. Instead they had proved themselves a capable, gritty sorority who stood by their own. I was now a bit in awe of those women.

Guilt

I remember returning home with Willow that day, and slumping in my chair, my fingers sunk in my collie's thick fur, and thinking how brief and terrible life could be. I wondered if the children's father, Bob Piero, really was abusive and bipolar, as Peggy and the other moms had said, or if those were just things the bus stop mothers had repeated out of anger. If he was, I wondered what would become of those two kids. I thought about Calista's pretty little daughter, Tessa, who had the same huge pale blue-green eyes as her mother, and the same gorgeous dark skin. I occasionally caught glimpses of this striking girl around our neighborhood because she often hung out after school with Peggy's daughter and another girl who lived close by us on the point.

It didn't occur to me at this juncture to think about Calista's little white dog. Actually, by the time she died, Calista's family had two dogs, Sadie the tiny Maltese, who was then around three, and a big overweight and wildly affectionate Golden Retriever named "Bandit," whom I had never met. At any rate, I was in such shock over the news about Calista that little Sadie never really crossed my mind.

The dogs didn't come onto my radar until a couple of months later. In the meanwhile, the Pieros' house went on the market, and we heard that Bob Piero was building the family a big new home over in Norwell, the next town inland from Marshfield. The Pieros, too, were moving to a "better" school district, which was a dance a lot of South Shore families did as their kids approached high school age—trying to pick the school district that would give their kids the best shot at a good college—the right athletic program or arts program, or whatever. Bob Piero was also, as I have said, bent on getting his kids out of the house where their mother had died. Nobody could fault him for this; it was certainly understandable. But Peggy and the other bus stop mothers worried that Tessa would be taken away from her pals in our neighborhood—yet another loss for this poor young girl.

So that was where things stood.

Then, later in the spring of 2002, I was out walking Willow to the point on a breezy, sunny morning, when I saw two dogs approaching who appeared to be running loose, unescorted by anyone. One was a big heavy-set Golden Retriever, and he was being shadowed by a tiny tan-colored dog with short frizzy hair. A toy poodle perhaps?

I had just bumped into my friend Melissa Raymond's husband, Paul Raymond, who was also headed out to the point with Melissa's Schnauzer, Echo, and the two of us had stopped to chat. Melissa was my closest friend in our neighborhood, and our two dogs—Echo and Willow—were pals, and had attended dog training classes together. Paul and I let our dogs socialize while we kept an eye on the two loose dogs. By this time the dogs, one large and one small, were getting closer to us and were ducking in and out of the marsh grass flanking the road.

"Do you think they're lost?" I asked Paul, a trim precise man with thinning hair. At this point I didn't recognize either of the loose dogs.

"I don't know," Paul said, and he shrugged. He didn't recognize them either, and we stood watching the dogs as they wandered over to sniff at our dogs, both of whom were on leashes.

The four dogs greeted each other in a friendly manner. The big Golden threw himself against my legs, seeking affection, while the little dog raced around the outside of the group. I still didn't recognize her as Sadie—partly because she was showing no interest in attacking Willow. She was also extremely skittish. She fled the moment we tried to catch her. But Paul and I were easily able to corral the fat Golden and get a look at his collar.

Paul read his tag. "Bandit," he said aloud. "There's a number but no owner name."

"Oh, you know," I said slowly, "these might be the Pieros' dogs." The name Bandit must have registered dimly somewhere in my memory, so perhaps I had heard it before.

"Maybe," Paul said. He looked doubtful.

We weren't sure.

I remember looking at the tiny dog and realizing at last that there was a chance this might be Sadie. It was hard to believe. If this was Sadie, somebody had cut off most of her long white fur and dyed it brown. Actually, her hair color was hard to tell because she was very dirty, probably from running around in the marshes with Bandit. And she had huge dark circles under her eyes, making her look sad and waifish. She seemed fit enough, though, and was having no trouble keeping up with her big friend, and was mirroring his every move, taking three steps for his every one. The main thing that suggested this might be Sadie, other than the name of her companion, was her diminutive size. It was now three years since I had first met her, but you still didn't see a lot of dogs around our neighborhood quite that small.

"A teensy dog shouldn't be running around loose like that," I remarked to Paul. She was likely to be eaten by a coyote or a hawk—predators we had lots of in Marshfield.

You always heard about cats and small dogs being snatched from people's backyards.

"And you don't want either of them getting hit by a car," Paul said.

Paul and I still couldn't catch the tiny dog, so we decided to lead Bandit away and see if she would follow. Paul didn't want to take the dogs back to his house because his wife Melissa is an enormous soft touch where dogs are concerned, and Paul said, "If they are the Pieros' dogs, and I take them home, she'll just wind up keeping them."

Paul's words would later seem prophetic.

We decided instead to take the two dogs back to my house, which was closer anyway. I would keep them in my kitchen while we tried to figure out if these were indeed the Pieros' dogs, and tried to get in touch with the family, or with the Town's animal control officer. Meanwhile, Paul would walk up to the Pieros' house, which was on his way home, and see if anyone was up there.

Looking back on this today, I can't account for why I so easily agreed to take the dogs into my home. Clearly I could have leaned on Paul, and he almost surely would have taken them home himself. Things could have gone either way.

The truth is, I think that I was still feeling guilty about Calista. I hadn't reached out to her when she was alive. But if her dogs were now in trouble, well, that I could do something about.

Chapter 4

"I NEEDED TO DO SOMETHING"

We led Bandit off by his collar to my house, and the tiny dog—whom I would later confirm was indeed Sadie—followed along behind us, just as we had hoped. The little dog appeared determined not to be left behind. I had a baby gate at home that I used to fence Willow in my kitchen while we were away, and I used it now to gate Bandit and the tiny dog in the kitchen, and to shut Willow out in the living room—at least until we could figure out whose two dogs these were. I didn't want Willow being exposed to any diseases by strange dogs.

There was nobody answering the phone number on Bandit's collar, so Paul went off to check the Pieros' house to see if anyone was at home there, while I began what would turn into a flurry of phone calls, to various neighbors and the animal control officer, and to Melissa and Paul when Paul finally made it back to their house. Between us, we pieced together the following information:

Yes, these were Calista Piero's dogs, Sadie and Bandit. However, nobody was home at the Pieros' house because Bob Piero was away on vacation with his new girlfriend and the two kids. There was a realtor who was supposed to be looking after the dogs, and coming by a couple of times a day to feed them and to let them out to do their business. But apparently at some point this realtor hadn't been able to get the dogs back in the house, and they had been outside running loose for at least one night, possibly two. No wonder little Sadie was so dirty.

My friends Paul and Melissa and some of our other neighbors were now making phone calls to try and get hold of the Pieros. After a bit of effort, I finally got Marshfield Animal Control on the line, and explained the situation. I asked if they couldn't take the dogs off my hands. I told them that I already had a dog, and didn't need two more. An overworked sounding woman on the other end of the line said the shelter was already brimful of cats and dogs, and that I would have to put the two dogs up myself until the Pieros could reclaim them. "Sorry," she said. "I can't help you."

For a time it appeared as if I might have the dogs for several days, though it turned out to be only a few hours. By early afternoon, a friend of the Piero family appeared to take them away. In the intervening period that I had the dogs in my kitchen, they both seemed very hungry and tired after their night (or two) out. I gave them water and some of Willow's food, and cut many burrs out of Bandit's shaggy coat. Little Sadie was plainly exhausted, but the excitable Bandit was having trouble settling down on the soft towels I provided. He kept jumping up and sniffing, and looking around rather desperately for more food—as if he would have to go yet again without his dinner. You could see from his pudgy figure that he was a real chowhound, and he loved his kibble.

"I Needed To Do Something"

At last Sadie appeared to be fed up with him. She trudged over and stood directly in front of the big Golden, and glared at him. Bandit dipped his head to one side, averting his eyes from this bossy little dog, but she issued a low growl from her throat. As I watched, surprised, Bandit dropped obediently to his belly and lay down for her, one rear leg kicked out to the side. Then Sadie—calm and utterly self-contained in her short muddy fur—climbed slowly up Bandit's outstretched leg and onto his broad, well-padded back, where she circled twice, lay down, and went to sleep.

I watched this little performance, astonished. It was exactly as if Sadie had brought into my kitchen her own personal, well-stuffed and heated sofa, and a portable one at that. It was the second time I had seen this tiny Maltese subdue a much larger dog. Unlike the previous time, though, when she had attacked Willow, this time my heart went out to her.

Here was this tiny toy dog who used to be someone's pampered pet. And now Calista was gone, and this poor little soul was bereft and dirty, and left out all night, nobody taking care of her—and yet she was still so utterly self-possessed and scrappy and bent on self-preservation. And now that she had eaten, she knew her big pal Bandit was, for her, a big soft heated dog-bed after a cold night out in the marshes.

The two dogs slept like that for a couple of hours, the little dog resting atop the big dog. By the time they were picked up, I was a big fan of little Sadie. I admired her spirit and grit, and I worried about what she was going back to, and whether she'd be taken care of. She didn't look like she was doing very well. I don't remember worrying too much about Bandit. He seemed big and dumb and durable, and as if he would get along okay. Sadie, though—despite her bossy resourcefulness—seemed tiny and fragile and sad.

I tried not to think about it. They weren't my dogs. It really wasn't any of my business. I didn't know Bob Piero at all. After three years, his kids would barely be recognizable as the children we had know from the bus stop—kids grew up so fast these days. I was going to give the dogs back, and stay out of it.

That was what I thought. That was my plan.

Interestingly, I don't remember picking Sadie up or cuddling her that morning in my kitchen. In fact, I don't recall ever holding her in my arms. While I admired her, and was worried about her, and while I hoped things would work out for her, I still had no interest in fondling or comforting a tiny dog like that. This probably seems a bit cold and heartless on my part, but as I have said, I had never liked small dogs and had no experience with them. The ones I had met were almost uniformly aggressive. And Sadie's attacks on Willow were still at the back of my mind.

So, while I felt for Sadie, and was determined to do for her what I could, it seemed as if we would all be better off if I just let her curl up with Bandit, rather than further traumatizing her by trying to cuddle her, and possibly expose myself to being bitten in the process. I was, in short, still far from scooping up this prickly little dog in my arms, let alone trying to claim her as my own.

It certainly looked to me as if the Piero dogs were beginning to suffer from neglect following Calista's death. Sadie's

"I Needed To Do Something"

hacked-off coat and dirty unkempt condition seemed more than could be explained merely by a couple of nights out in the marsh. Still, after returning Sadie and Bandit, I wasn't inclined to judge Bob Piero for the way he was running his household. He no doubt had his hands full, I thought. He now had complete responsibility for two growing kids, a business to run, a house to sell, and a move to negotiate. It was hardly surprising that his boarding arrangements for the dogs were less than stellar. Or that he hadn't gotten around to getting them groomed.

Also, I wasn't really in a position to offer to take Sadie and Bandit myself, even on a provisional basis, even if I was inclined to do so, which I wasn't. We already had Willow and a very elderly cat, and our house wasn't that big. Also, Willow—though he was only three—had been diagnosed with advanced arthritis, probably as a result of being too highly-bred. So I already had ownership of a large dog in less than optimal health. I simply wasn't a good candidate to take in two more neglected dogs, even if the Piero family could be convinced to part with them—hardly a sure bet at the time. The Piero kids had just lost their mother. I couldn't imagine that the adults around them would want to take away their dogs, too.

Sadie must have been on my mind, though, because a couple of months later—this was now about six months after Calista's death and the beginning of the summer of '02—I remember that I was driving down the main road from the point to do some errands, and I passed our old bus stop just down the hill from where the Pieros lived—and I saw out of the corner of my eye a little white dog running loose in the bushes at the side of the road. I was sure it was Sadie.

Did I really see Sadie that day?

I was pretty sure at the time that it was her. However, I later learned that another family in the same area had gotten a white toy poodle of about the same size, and that they often let it run around loose. So it's possible that it was that dog I saw that day, and not Sadie.

In any event, I was in a hurry and kept driving, and I didn't stop for a closer look. But I certainly thought that I'd seen Sadie out running loose again, this time all by herself. I remember thinking, *Not again*. I remember being mad at myself for not stopping. And mad at the Pieros for letting this tiny fragile creature out unsupervised yet again—this time without even Bandit for company—to be hit by a car, or stolen, or devoured by a coyote.

In fact, I got downright angry at the Pieros. Too angry. Angrier than I should have been.

Why was I so angry?

The reason is something that I can only appreciate now, in the cool light of hindsight. In addition to the survivor guilt I surely felt, this whole situation with the Pieros dogs was bringing back a similar trauma I had experienced when I was not much older than the Piero kids, after my own father had died.

When I was about twelve or thirteen, my father was in a car accident late one evening coming home from a business trip in New York City. The brakes on his car failed on a rural road not far from our home, and he hit a tree. He didn't die instantly but suffered severe head injuries, and lingered in a coma for six months in the hospital before he passed away. Our family went through the same kind of shock and transition that the Piero family was now going through, and, I have to say, the whole situation felt way too familiar to me.

"I Needed To Do Something"

And here's the kicker, the thing that was really setting off my alarm bells—In the aftermath of this horror with my father, we had a family dog that we also neglected, with fatal consequences.

The dog we had at the time was a female German Shepherd, named Chloe. She was young and aggressive, and a real behavior problem. If someone had been paying attention to her, and training her, I'm sure that she easily could have been whipped into shape. She was a gorgeous, athletic young dog, and very smart and responsive. But in our grief-stricken state after my father's death, we neglected her.

We let Chloe run around loose in our suburban neighborhood, when she should have been fenced or tied. She got into all sorts of trouble. She broke into people's garbage, chased the neighbor kids, occasionally bit people—yes, she actually bit our neighbors—none of which our stunned family did anything about, or even especially seemed to take notice of. It was as if we were immobilized, frozen. When you are traumatized that way, you shut down.

Eventually someone fed Chloe rat poison. Actually, I suppose it's possible the poisoning was accidental, since she was going through people's garbage—though I have always believed that one of the neighbors finally took things into his own hands and put an end to this canine menace.

In any event, Chloe came home and threw up half the blood in her body on the floor of our garage. It was a horrible way to die. And all that congealed blood pooled on the cold concrete floor of our garage still scars my memory today. Strangely, I remember this little scene far more vividly than the other details attending my father's death—about which I recall very little. I seem to have blocked out most of that period in my mind.

I don't think I was aware that the situation with the Pieros and their dogs was pushing this visceral button in my brain, not at least until later, but I do recall getting far too worked up about seeing Sadie out running loose again that day. It seemed terribly irresponsible to me. It also seemed that I had to do something about it immediately, *or Sadie would almost certainly wind up dead*—a conclusion which (though it turned out to be true) was a stretch given my level of knowledge at the time.

And so I asked our dog walker, a woman named Josie Campbell, to check up on how the Piero dogs were doing, and to ask in a low-key sort of way whether the family was planning to keep them.

We had hired Josie a year earlier to walk Willow, once we found out that he had bad arthritis at such a young age. Half the battle with an arthritic dog lies in simply keeping him moving. So we hired Josie to come in at midday and take Willow out for walks, and to keep him entertained and happy while we were working and while Dan was at school. Josie was a real dog lover, and she stuffed Willow with treats, and played with him, and he adored her. She also often brought over other dogs she walked to play with Willow in our yard. These dogs included a particularly lively and clownish Jack Russell terrier puppy. The Jack was small and light enough that he could play with Willow without hurting my collie's sore joints, unlike some of the larger dogs we knew. Willow and the Jack would chase each other around the yard, and then collapse and roll about on the lawn, tussling and nipping. It was hilarious to watch. A real dog-circus. Perhaps it

"I Needed To Do Something"

was this pairing that first suggested to my mind that Willow might benefit from a smaller companion.

In any event, I told Josie of my concerns about the Piero dogs, and of seeing Sadie running loose again, and I asked her to check on them. Josie, who walked a number of dogs on our street, was always around the neighborhood, and she was delighted to take on the assignment. A retired flight attendant, she liked talking to people, and was something of a busybody (as I myself apparently was becoming).

Being in the animal care business, Josie considered it something of her self-appointed duty to make sure no dogs in her part of town were being neglected, and that they were all walked and happy. She also may have been hunting for new business and thinking that the Pieros might hire her to walk their dogs for them. At any rate, she was more than happy to make inquiries while doing her daily dog-walking rounds.

The last thing I remember saying to Josie as she went out the door that day was, "If they want to get rid of Sadie, tell Bob Piero I'll take her." For reasons that I didn't yet fully understand, I was now firmly bent on rescuing Sadie if she needed rescuing.

I should say here that I still had no intention of keeping the tiny Maltese, though I was intensely worried about her fate. The last time I'd seen her, Sadie had been a shadow of her former self—her regal white coat hacked off, cold and muddy, and with big circles under her eyes. I would fix her up, I thought. I would keep her for awhile, a few months or whatever it took to get her back to being the pretty little princess she used to be when Calista had her. And then she'd be easy to place in a good home. In the condition she was in, nobody would want her. They would see only a pile of vet bills.

So my mission was one of repair, not adoption. I would save Sadie, I thought, and then I would give her away. Meanwhile, I would see how Willow liked living with a smaller canine companion. I doubted, based on their history, that Willow and Sadie would ever get along. And I still had no intention of ever owning a shrill little lap dog, but I thought that one of the smaller terrier breeds might eventually be nice. A Westie or a Cairn, perhaps, or a Jack Russell terrier like the one Willow played with.

I don't think the reality of what I had just offered—to take Sadie—had quite sunk into my brain, though, because I remember taking a big gulp of air and swallowing hard when I got a note back from Josie the next afternoon, a Tuesday afternoon. The note started something like, *You can have Sadie. Call Bob Piero about picking her up . . . .*

Josie, it turned out, had talked to the Pieros, and they were moving to a rental house for six months while they were waiting for their new place in Norwell to be finished. The rental didn't allow pets, and so they needed to find homes for the two dogs right away. Another family had already offered to take Bandit. Josie had written down the number where Bob Piero could be reached after work.

Things were suddenly moving much faster than I had anticipated, and I had one of those "What am I doing?" moments. I guess I felt a bit helpless in the face of the situation. I felt I needed to rescue Sadie. *I needed to do something.*

"I Needed To Do Something"

When I called Bob Piero on the phone that evening, he sounded perfectly nice, but overwhelmed and tired, as you might expect. He repeated the line I had heard from Josie about "moving to a rental that didn't allow pets." He said Sadie was "a nice little dog" but admitted they were having trouble caring for the two dogs with Calista gone. We made plans for me to pick up Sadie on Thursday after school, "when the kids could say goodbye."

When I saw Josie the next day—I was around when she came to take Willow out for his daily walk—she put a darker spin on things. She'd been up to the Piero house twice now, and had seen Sadie, and she was a wreck. I was getting her just in time, she said.

Sadie had been peeing on the carpets while they were trying to sell the house, so they were keeping her crated in the basement while Bob Piero was at work and the kids were at school. Sadie was sitting down there in the cold basement all day long, in her own urine, and she was dirty and skinny and had sores on her bottom. One of her arms was shaved, Josie said, because she'd gotten dehydrated, and the Pieros had to take her to the vet for administration of intravenous fluids.

Josie was furious at the treatment of this little dog, and was in full rescue mode, her face glowing with the urgency of her mission.

If there was any chance I might have backed out until this moment—which in my mind there still was—this awful news sealed the deal. Sadie's situation was fully as serious as I had guessed. There would be no turning back now. Especially not with Josie on a tear—her face alight with animal rescue fervor.

There was something else, too, something I hadn't counted on when I asked Josie to intervene: My son Daniel's reaction.

I hadn't thought my son would care about a little lap dog. He was a boy, and boys didn't like tiny shrill dogs, right? I mean, this was a little girl's dog, not a boy's dog. But Daniel was a sensitive excitable third grader, and like most kids that age, he loved animals, especially dogs. When Dan heard that we were getting a little white jumpy dog, he got so excited that he himself began to bounce and vibrate. All I had to do was say the words "little white jumpy dog" and his imagination ran away with him.

My son was now spending all of his time drawing sketches of cute little white dogs with curly coats across his big creamy sketchpads. And of course he demanded to go with me to "help pick up Sadie." I could hardly say no. It was suddenly starting to look as if we might be making a bigger commitment to this tiny lapdog than I had ever anticipated or wished. *(Oh, what would my mother think?)*

In retrospect, it's easy to see that I shouldn't have taken Daniel with me to pick up Sadie that sunny Thursday afternoon. Did I really think it would be smooth and painless to separate this little dog from two bereft children? What was I thinking? But at the time it seemed all set. Bob Piero had said they were moving to a new place that didn't allow pets. Surely the children had been told that they were going to have to give up their dogs.

I tried to play-down Daniel's expectations. "Don't expect her to look like much," I warned him. "I've heard she's not in good shape. And I'm not even sure we'll keep her. Let's see what she's like, and if she gets along with Willow okay.

Willow was here first." I reminded him of how Sadie used to attack Willow at the bus stop.

These words made absolutely no impression upon my son. He kept on drawing—more little white adorable dogs jumping up, rolling over, chasing tennis balls.

Chapter 5

IMPROMPTU RESCUE

That Thursday afternoon we pulled up the long drive toward the Pieros' big house, the wheels of our Subaru Outback popping the fine white gravel. It was easy to tell which of these mansions was theirs. There was a big "For Sale" sign out front for the same real estate agency where Calista used to work, and the grass around the house was long and untended, and the gardens overgrown. The whole scene had an air of disuse and neglect. And—was it my imagination?—The big grey house now appeared a bit haunted. The happiness and prosperity which this large new home had once seemed to promise had utterly evaporated, and the place now seemed like a great hollow shell, a mockery of a dream.

That's one of the problems with living large in the suburbs, or so I have since come to believe. Life catches up with all of us sooner or later, doesn't it? Our suburban lives, which often look so perfect from the outside, rarely stay that way for long—Our basements flood, our children disappoint, the people we love most fall ill or die. Yet the suburbs invite us to judge our neighbors (many of whom we barely know) from the intimate distance of our yards, and based upon the appearances of our homes and gardens. As we tend our lawns and paint our fences, we nearly always advertise the illusion of gracious living—a statement that is invariably to some extent false, if not doomed. It is something that I believe can make suburban living seem quite surreal and strange, despite its many comforts and amenities—and though it is often hard for suburban dwellers to imagine raising their children anywhere else.

Driving up to the Pieros' house that day, I had never felt quite so keenly this surreal sense of suburban doom.

Daniel, meanwhile, was bouncing excitedly on the backseat, and talking a mile a minute. As we drew up in front of the house, I was already wishing that I hadn't brought him with me. Josie's report about Sadie's condition had started to bring back memories of what had happened with Chloe long ago, giving me a deep sense of foreboding. We pulled to a stop in front of the big grey house, and I spied Calista's two kids. They were visible inside the cavernous three-car garage, games and toys and cardboard boxes strewn around them. Apparently they were packing to move.

We got out of the car, and Calista's son Robbie emerged from the dimness to greet us, blinking in a sheet of bright sunlight at the mouth of the garage. I recognized him from the bus stop, but he had been a little boy back then, and now he was a big lumpy budding-teenager of twelve or thirteen. Someday soon, I knew, he was likely to shoot up into a tall fellow, as handsome as his mother and sister. For the moment, however, he was trapped in that in-between stage boys go through in adolescence, and he looked fat and sullen. Losing his mother surely hadn't helped. "What do you want?" he demanded. His tone made Daniel edge behind me.

"We're here to pick up Sadie," I said. This statement came out a question.

"What are you talking about?" the boy said, his face reddening. I could tell from his reaction that he probably had been told something was happening today, though perhaps not the whole story.

"Your father talked to you about this," I said. Again, my statement seemed to come out a question.

"What did he say?"

"He said that you're going to be renting while you're waiting for your new house to be done, and that they don't allow pets. Isn't that right?" I could hear in my voice that bright gentle grownup's tone that no child should ever trust.

"That's right," I heard a girl's voice behind him. Calista's pretty daughter, Tessa, had come up behind her brother's shoulder. "They don't allow pets," she told him. "Dad said." Braces flashed on Tessa's teeth, and her voice held a note of antagonism for her older sibling.

Tessa, I realized suddenly, was mad at her brother for making a big deal out of this. It was only for six months, right? Nobody had told these kids that they were about to lose their dogs.

With his sister's validation of what their father had said, Robbie's face began turning back to a normal color, the ruddy hue draining out of it. Still, he didn't look happy. He glanced back at the house, as if for help he knew wasn't there. Then he said, "Just for six months."

"That's right," I agreed, smooth as silk. "Just for six months." What was I going to say? "In six months if you kids want Sadie back, you just say so, alright?"

"Whaaat?!" I heard Daniel's outraged cry behind me. I had forgotten about him. "You never said it was just for six months!"

Poor Daniel. From his perspective, something was very wrong here. Either I had failed to tell him that the little white jumpy dog I had promised was just for six months, or the dog was going to be permanent and he had just caught me lying to these poor bereft children. Either way, I was a lousy parent and a rotten human being, and he was going to let me have it. I would have to deal with him later, though. "Back in the car," I told him.

"But Mom!"

"Car."

Slowly, and with a huge pout thrusting out his lower lip, my son went back to our Outback and slid into the rear seat of the car, leaving the door slightly ajar so he could still hear what was happening.

By the time I turned back to the Piero kids, their father Bob Piero had come out of the house, to my enormous relief. We introduced ourselves. Bob seemed nice enough, as he had on the phone. He was an affable, businesslike fellow with thick black hair. I repeated that the children could have their dog back in six months if they wanted, once they were in their new home. I said I understood they were in transition.

"We'll see," Bob said, and I was left with the distinct impression that he had no plans to take the dog back. On the other hand, he also didn't say that the adoption was permanent, even after he sent his kids into the house to get Sadie.

I didn't press the issue. At that point I just wanted to get the dog, and leave. We could work out later whether or not she was coming back.

When the Piero kids returned, carrying Sadie, my worst fears were confirmed. She now looked less like a dog than a raw pink worm.

The tiny animal's white flaxen coat was utterly gone. What little fur she had left was matted into tiny dirty brown knots all over her body, almost as if it were trying to knit itself into tiny dreadlocks. And you could see right through the matted fur to her reddish-brown freckled skin and emaciated frame, her ribs visibly white and protruding. She had enormous dark circles under her eyes that I would later come to understand were tear-stains that need to be cleaned periodically in this type of dog to prevent the build-up of dark minerals. Sadie's eyes hadn't been cleaned in months. I didn't know all of this yet, and saw only two enormous black eyes with huge dark rings around them. The little dog looked like the posters of Cosette from *Les Miserables*. And she was shivering uncontrollably, waves of shivers seeming to pass through her body in pulses.

Any reluctance I'd had to take Sadie away from Calista's kids evaporated once I saw her. My instincts had been right. This was Chloe all over again. I now felt sick to my stomach, but at least it was clear what I needed to do. *Get this dog out of here!*

"Look, she can walk on my shoulders," the boy Robbie was saying. He said this both proudly and as if he might cry. He boosted Sadie up on his neck, and I watched half in horror as the pathetic pink waif-dog manfully scrambled about the boy's round shoulders on her tiny rat feet, her long black nails digging into his white T-shirt and soft flesh. She seemed to be doing her best to entertain the assembled—a sad little clown doing tricks. It was a heartbreaking performance to watch.

Bob Piero and I exchanged a few more words. It turned out that the dog slept every night with Robbie, so she should feel comfortable sleeping with Daniel. I told the kids that they could come and visit Sadie any time they wanted; we lived just down the road on the point.

"All right, that's enough," Bob Piero said at last. He plucked the dog briskly off his son's shoulders. He was plainly embarrassed by the dog's condition. He told the kids, "Say goodbye now and go back in the house." A note of harshness had entered his voice.

Suddenly everything began to happen very fast. Bob carried Sadie over to our car, opened the door to the backseat where Daniel was sitting, and tossed Sadie onto his lap, and then slammed the door. This left me free to climb back into the car myself. As I did, I heard a cry escape the mouth of Calista's beautiful daughter, Tessa, a cry like the flash of a fountain spouting in the air that seemed to emanate from the silver braces on her teeth. Then I saw Bob Piero trying to pull his son away from the car. The boy was shouting and trying to shove past his father to retrieve his dog from Daniel. Hastily I threw the Outback into reverse, and began pulling away. As the car began to move, I remember Robbie's fists raining down hard on the side of the car, a sharp knuckled sound, like hailstones hitting the car, and I remember Bob Piero wrapping his arms around the boy's waist from the rear and lifting his heavy figure into the air as easily as if he were made of Styrofoam.

I wanted in that moment mainly to get my own young son away from this large enraged teenager, and I recall that I pulled out a little too fast, the tires of the Outback spinning and slipping on the white gravel like a getaway car in a movie, fishtailing as we turned onto the main road.

As I straightened out the car and headed for home, I felt myself panting and heard Daniel crying a little in the backseat.

"I'm so sorry you had to see that," I told my son over my shoulder. "I should never have brought you."

There was silence from the backseat as we drove the short distance to our house, and I was sure that my son was scarred for life. But while I was driving, and trying to recover from the wrenching scene we had just witnessed, Sadie was busy nestling into Daniel's lap. By the time we reached home and pulled into our driveway, and I turned to look at them—expecting to see Daniel's stricken face—Sadie was fast asleep in his lap, though she was still shivering a little, and Dan was stroking her like they were old friends. I shut off the car and turned to look at them, and Sadie woke and raised her tiny head, and gazed at me with her enormous black waif eyes.

"Mom," Dan said, with that wonderful sustaining selfishness of children, "Do we really have to give her back in six months?" This question would become a common refrain at our house over the coming months.

"I don't know, honey," I said, reluctant to make any more promises to children that day that I couldn't keep.

It's hard to describe the mix of emotions I felt that afternoon. In addition to the sadness of the situation itself, I was also feeling something of the revisited excruciation of losing a parent, which had come flooding back upon me. The Piero kids had reminded me of those terrible feelings, still too close and familiar to me—of my mother's recent death and, of course, the horror of losing my father at thirteen, which was something I would never really get over. And then, too, there was the guilt of recognizing that I had survived all of that while the Piero kids were still wallowing in that awful emotional place.

There was also something unseemly in my suppressed glee at having gotten Sadie out of there—at assisting her grit and determination to survive. I think, looking back on it, that I was oddly relating way too much to Sadie and her fight to live. It was strange—that some ways I would relate more to the dog than to the kids—but I had once survived a parent's loss myself, and I think I was re-living that drama of survival through the rescue of this little dog.

And blended somewhere into this strange brew of feelings was my sorrow for Bob Piero. He had been vilified by the bus stop mothers, but he was going through something that would have been just awful for any parent. He was dealing, day to day, with two children who had recently lost their mother. I could still see him in my mind lifting his son into the air. There was something so eloquent in that gesture, that lifting up of his half-grown child. It said that he had been—for whatever his faults—an involved father, and that he had probably lifted his son up a million times before like that. And, not so long ago, maybe just last year, his son had been a little boy. But now Bob Piero was lifting this big lumpy teenager, trying to control him, trying to subdue him, trying probably even to comfort him.

But how could you assuage all of that sadness, all of that rage the boy surely felt over losing his mother? And at the divorce that had preceded her death?

You couldn't, I thought. You couldn't comfort him, and you couldn't make it better. You could only live day to day, and try to get through it.

After we got home, Dan went up to his room to play video games, and I sat on the couch, holding Sadie on my lap to keep her warm, and had a good cry.

After awhile, the tears dried. Somehow, we had both survived, both Sadie and me. And the Piero kids would, too. I was pretty sure of it. The boy's anger was a good sign, I knew. I was actually a little more worried about Tessa, who still appeared to be in a state of total denial about what was happening with the dogs. I feared (correctly, as it turned out) that it wouldn't be the last we would see of her.

After I had recovered a bit, I picked Sadie up in my arms and brought her to the kitchen, and gave her some water and some wet dog food, which I let her lick off my fingers.

Then I found a pair of blunt-tipped fingernail scissors in a kitchen drawer, and took her back to the couch, and began working on her—cutting away all of the tiny knots in what little remaining hair she had left, trying to leave as much fur as possible until she could grow back a better coat. As I worked, I felt the sharp curved ribs of her emaciated frame against my hands—like one of Daniel's plastic dinosaur models—and the bite of her overgrown toenails, like tiny black thistle seeds, digging into my knees, and the unaccustomed feather weight of her in my lap.

As we sat there together, Sadie grew warmer and more relaxed, and her incessant shivering gradually slowed and then, finally, ceased. I remember thinking, as if this were a revelation, *Oh, so that's why they call them lap dogs.* They are small and they need a lap to sit on to stay warm.

It was my first real encounter with this new kind of dog, about which I knew so little, and had so much to learn.

Chapter 6

SEPARATION ANXIETY

After we took possession of Sadie, the next few weeks appear in my memory as a blur of repeating vet clinic visits—strobing flashes of examining rooms lit in quick succession by too-bright florescent lights. Sadie, it turned out, was harboring worms, had a raging urinary tract infection, and was severely malnourished. The first vet we saw declared that she was "digesting her own muscle" to stay alive, and that her body had "wasted." Her weight, which previously had hovered between six and eight pounds when Calista had her, had now sunk below four and was still dropping.

We decided that the Pieros must have been feeding the two dogs together, and that pudgy Bandit had probably been vacuuming up most of the food before Sadie could get her share. I have also since come to believe that Sadie was just terribly sad at losing Calista, and that she probably didn't have much of an appetite.

I tried not to think about it, but I knew that the little dog must have spent day after day in bed with a dying woman, trying to heal and comfort her as best she knew how, not knowing how, while her owner grew sicker and sicker. A loyal companion to the end. It must have been a sadness beyond reckoning, even for an animal.

And then, after all of that, to be left alone and neglected, as she had been, in a crate down in the basement. It was amazing to me that her little spirit had kept flickering inside of her.

Sadie's awful condition was made worse by the fact that, due to malnourishment, her teeth had gotten very loose, which made eating difficult for her. Little dogs are famous for having bad teeth, and Sadie's were a wreck. We ended up having to pull most of her front teeth, which were too compromised to save. For the rest of her life, the slip of her long pink tongue would poke out the front of her mouth, like a stuffed animal's tongue, because she lacked the teeth to hold it in.

Steve and Daniel decided to take Sadie's dreadful condition as hilarious, and spent a lot of time making fun of her to mask the shock of how awful she looked. "Oh you cute little drowned rat you," Dan would tease her, as he cuddled her to him. "Oh, put your tongue back in your mouth you poor skinny old thing!"

Sadie would immediately climb into the lap of whoever sat down in the living room, which happened conveniently to be where Dan flopped to have his snacks after school. It was also where Steve collapsed on the couch and ate dinner every night in front of the television after a long day at the law office.

Sadie was so emaciated that both male members of our household quickly got into the routine of, one bite for me, one bite for Sadie. I didn't quite approve of these new habits, or of eating with a dog on one's lap, but Sadie was so skinny and pathetic that at first hand-feeding her seemed necessary and appropriate. What I didn't appreciate, of course, was that once established, these habits would be well nigh impossible to break. At the time, though, we weren't thinking that far ahead.

As Sadie began her slow recovery, my most immediate concern was what to do with her in the moments when I couldn't be sitting with her on the couch, holding her in my lap. I was starting to enjoy my own "cuddle time" with this little waif. However, I did have things to do. But the moment I made to leave the house, or even go upstairs to work in my office, Sadie would fly into a state of deep anxiety and consternation.

She would begin an incessant crying howl, Yow, yow, yow, her body stiffening and quaking. She would attempt to block my exit with her small hairless body, and, if I managed to get past her, she would grasp my pants leg with what few remaining teeth she had, and hang on for dear life.

I didn't realize it at the time, but apparently separation anxiety is quite common in rescued dogs, and is a natural response to having the dog's usual "pack relationships" disrupted, which makes the dog feel highly vulnerable. Among wolves and other wild canids, such "pack abandonment" often spells doom. As a result, rescued dogs will glue themselves onto whomever they perceive as being the "senior" members of their new pack-family, and they exhibit anxiety, if not outright panic, when left alone.

All of this was of course complicated in Sadie's case by her loss of Calista. Having just watched her old "momma" expire before her eyes, and disappear, she seemed almost frantic not to let that happen again. She was determined not to let me—her "new momma"—out of her sight. Sadie's separation anxiety was certainly understandable, but it was terrible to see this pathetic, shivering creature fall to into such hysterics. When I took Willow outside to do his business, I could still hear her screeching inside the house, ever more shrilly, with her high-pitched yow, yow, yow.

What was I going to do? I had a household to run, and a child to raise. Willow needed to be walked regularly. And at that point I was in the middle of writing and researching a book, as well as teaching writing workshops in the city two nights a week.

Sadie actually seemed to do okay if I left her at night, since I could usually hand her off to Steve or Daniel, who kept her snuggled and happy. During the day, though, there was nobody else around.

Well, that's not quite accurate. Willow was around.

I guess I had been counting on Willow to keep Sadie company during the day. But poor Willow was proving no help at all. A mere two or three days into her recovery, Sadie had gotten enough of her strength back to start attacking my big collie again. When I wasn't sitting on the couch with Sadie, the little dog would stand guard on the spot where I usually sat, defending this treasured place as if her very life depended on it. If Willow got anywhere near the couch Sadie would begin growling and snapping at him.

Poor Willow, he was incensed. Previously, he had been the top dog, and had full run of the house. Now here he was, being chased off from the place where everyone sat by this naked mole rat. He plainly felt banished and insulted. Soon he wouldn't even enter the living room.

He exiled himself to a rug in the foyer by the front door with an air of dignified and shocked disgust. When anyone came in or out of the front door, he would try and flee to his tie-out in the front yard under a large pine tree. So much for hoping that the two dogs would be companions, I thought. So much for hoping they would get along.

I needed some sort of strategy, that much was clear. It didn't seem as if I could just leave this tiny half-bare dog howling at home while I went out. And poor Willow clearly needed a break. I was beginning to have sympathy for the Pieros, and to understand why they had kept the little dog crated while they were away during the day.

I went on the Internet and did some research about what to do for separation anxiety. The advice I got said that, since Sadie previously had a stable home, she would probably calm down once she settled into her new environs—and once she was convinced she wouldn't be abandoned again. In the meanwhile, I could expect the "panic behaviors" associated with separation anxiety to include all manner of bad behavior, such as howling, urinating and defecating in the house, "shredding" garbage and other household objects, and sometimes desperate attempts to "escape" confinement alone in the house—something these rescued dogs view as dangerous to their very lives.

The animal behaviorists I was reading said that the main thing a rescued dog needed was kind and firm leadership. Several suggested leashing the dog to you, and taking it everywhere with you, until good habits and predictable schedules could be reestablished.

Sadie, with her scrawny pink chicken's neck, was hardly a good candidate to be dragged about by a collar and leash. So I did the next best thing that I could think of. I started "wearing" her around, the way I used to wear Daniel when he was a new baby and I was nursing.

At first I tried wearing Sadie in Dan's old "baby sling," but it worked better just to tuck her inside whatever shirt or jacket I happened to have on. I had been holding Sadie on my lap a lot, but this was a whole new level of intimacy with this tiny dog. Her little paws would find purchase on my chest or bra, and her tiny head would poke out the throat of my collar. We went around that way for a number of weeks, while Sadie was too weak to get down and walk by herself, and too nervous to be left behind at home. Wherever we went, there was her little round dog head bobbing under my chin. Driving out for supplies; taking Willow to the dog park; picking up Dan at school—We must have looked quite ridiculous. A human with two heads.

Wearing Sadie around was, in truth, a lot like wearing around a small baby. And I have to admit, I loved it. I think that I missed having my "baby Daniel" around, now that my son was growing up and was spending most of his day in school, or, in the summer, at camp. And, as much as my mother would have cringed to hear me say it, I enjoyed the creature-warmth and intimacy of toting around my "new baby." The effect on Sadie was almost magical. Cuddled against me, she was relaxed and rather sleepy, yet attentive.

When she wanted to get down and do her business or smell something, Sadie would begin to struggle a little, and I would feel her tiny paws kicking my front, just the way I remembered Dan's feet kicking me when he was an infant in his sling, asking to be fed. Only now there were four legs thumping my belly and chest, instead of two.

When she started to squirm, I would set Sadie down on the ground. She would sniff and pee. Then, when she was done, she would look back up at me and utter a sharp bark, asking to be picked up again. She was still too weak to walk much, but she seemed to like being out and about, seeing the world. She was so small that most people didn't even detect that I had her snuggled in my jacket, so we often managed to go places where dogs weren't really allowed, such as coffee shops or the grocery store.

Steve and Daniel were usually away at work or at school while I was carrying Sadie around in this fashion. However, a few times on the weekends they caught sight of me cuddling her under my shirt, her head poking up beneath my chin, and they snorted loudly and rolled their eyes.

Daniel proclaimed me "weird." "You're weird, Mom," he would say. "Really strange." (Was he a little jealous of the attention that I was lavishing on this tiny canine?)

I would have to remind Dan and his father that I wasn't the one who was sharing *my every meal* with this newest member of our household.

Many of my earliest trips out with Sadie were for purposes of walking Willow at conservation areas. We had a dog walker during the day, as I have said. However, Willow still needed walking mornings and evenings, and he and I had gotten into the habit of meeting up early each morning with a group of dogs and their owners to go hiking at a nature preserve across the river, in Scituate, Massachusetts.

This nature area boasted a long, lovely pathway through heather-fringed dunes, and in the early summer the whole area was fragrant with the lemony-scent of beach roses. We would stroll out through the dunes with our doggie playgroup, to a marsh meadow that gave onto a view of the river, where we could let the dogs loose to run and tussle.

I remember the first time I got out of my car, and had to explain to this group of other dog walkers the tiny head bobbing under my chin. The others all had dogs of varying sizes and breeds, but all of the dogs were upwards of thirty-five pounds, and most were the sorts of active breeds that required constant vigorous exercise—which was the main point of these outings. At the time, our group included, in addition to Willow, two manic Golden Retrievers, a couple of Border Collie mixes, a fleet Eskimo dog, and a speed-demon lowland sheepdog that made the Border Collies look slow by comparison, if you can imagine. These dogs raced about, biting and wrestling at high speed, occasionally threatening to slam into you if you weren't careful to ward them off.

When I got out of my car with Sadie that first morning, you could see the other dog owners shaking their heads a little, and wondering audibly how this tiny pink worm wedged in my jacket was ever going to fit into our active playgroup. My friend Erin remembers thinking that Sadie was in such bad condition that she "wouldn't live."

One of our friends, a tall Dutch engineer named Frits—and the fellow who owned the lowland sheepdog—leaned over to peer at Sadie, and wrinkled up his nose. He said in his Germanic-sounding accent, as if questioning my sanity, "What are you doing? It's not even a dog."

"It's a rescue," I explained. "I'm just fixing the poor thing up."

Frits didn't look convinced and muttered something about naked hamsters. As we walked, he kept glancing back at the little head poking up at my throat, with its slip of pink tongue hanging out, his face registering what appeared to be disapproval, or perhaps disgust.

"Once she's feeling better, I'm going to give her away," I offered.

I'm not sure why I said this. It was already starting to be a lie. This was a line I would continue repeating for another month or two, although it was already becoming pretty clear that our family probably wasn't going to want to part with Sadie, not unless the Piero kids insisted on taking her back. I think that I was keeping up this line at least partly to try and let myself off the hook with friends like Frits, who couldn't quite imagine why I was taking on a project like Sadie, when so much of our lives with our dogs at the time involved brisk walking outside at conservation areas.

We usually went places full of mud and brush and rough, twisted terrain. Hawks, coyotes and other predators lurked about, ready to devour small animals that came by. A tiny lapdog like Sadie just didn't seem to match our lifestyle. She appeared at that point to be exclusively an indoor dog, tiny, shivering, nearly hairless, her feet barely ever grazing the ground. Adopting her must have seemed to my friends, not only like an enormous undertaking—she was such a mess—but also something of a betrayal of our troop.

Sadie was also probably changing the group's view of me in rather substantial ways—something I didn't fully appreciate at the time. This dog-walking crowd had always known me as a big-dog person, escorting about a tall, gorgeous collie, and hiking for hours. Now here I was with this delicate, babyish creature squirming in my blouse. Who was this person they called their friend? It was like they didn't know me anymore.

Little did I know at the time that my friends were actually biting back the worst of their comments—The true strength of their opinions would come out only later, when I would hear things like, "Kim, you were the LAST person we expected to show up with a tiny rat-dog." Or, "To be completely honest, we sort of thought you were losing your mind."

The strong reactions Sadie provoked from my dog walking pals, and would elicit from my other friends, surprised me at first. I hadn't realized that anyone would especially care what kind of dog I had, or that they might take it personally. But, of course, I should have realized that the very same sorts of judgments my mother and I had once applied to our neighbors with the Pom would now be applied to me.

In fairness to my friends, I should add here that, despite whatever initial reluctance they may have had to accept Sadie into our midst, she soon became a regular member of our morning playgroup. It wasn't long before everyone was petting her, and handing her around, and taking care to shield her from the antics of the big dogs. And of course everyone had to slip her tidbits of dog treats and any human breakfast that had been brought along—in order to "fatten her up," or so they said. So even this outdoorsy set was not entirely resistant to the charms of a tiny lapdog.

Still, there was always a sense in the air of "not quite sure" about Sadie, particularly among the men. Something that said that I was trying to change the unwritten rules of our clan.

Chapter 7

A BRAND NEW DOG

By the time a few weeks had elapsed, Sadie was already looking a lot better. She had been treated for worms, and had finished her round of antibiotics for her urinary tract infection. She was beginning to put some weight back on her tiny frame, and was already sprouting new tufts of white fur and shedding out her old knotted brown coat.

I had also been working on the tear stains around her eyes, and trying to do something about them as well, though with limited success. Never having had a little lapdog before, I had to read up on tear stains, and what the story was with them. Apparently tear stains are caused by poor eye-drainage in these smaller breeds of dog, such as Poodles, Bichon Frise and Maltese. This results in a build-up of yeasts and bacteria around the eyes which produce rust-colored "porphyrin" pigments (iron-based pigments), stains that are particularly visible on light and white-coated dogs.

There are actually a number of commercial products for cleaning tear stains, with names like "Angel Eyes" and "Angel's Glow." These commercial products contain antibiotics and other chemicals meant to prevent or break up porphyrin stains. However, the products I tried on Sadie were all quite foamy and sudsy, and they seemed to irritate her eyes. I often found them as hard to wash away as the tear stains themselves.

Also, by the time we got her, Sadie's tear stains were much more than just "stains." Her eyes had gone unattended for so long that the pigments and bacteria had built up into solid crusts all around the bottoms of her eyes. Underneath the crusts there were raw patches of flesh that had become irritated by the build-up. When I tried to wash the stains away, or pluck off the crusted matter, I would end up taking tender, inflamed skin and fur with it.

The only way to begin dealing with Sadie's tear stains seemed to be by slowly softening the crusts under her eyes with warm water, and then gently cleaning them away with a warm, damp cotton ball. It was a slow and laborious process, and seemed to be taking forever. Eventually, in frustration, I decided to get some professional help. I ended up taking Sadie to the same grooming salon where I took Willow to have his thick collie undercoat stripped out several times a year.

Here I ran into a bit of good luck. I quickly discovered that this was the same place where Calista used to take Sadie and Bandit to be groomed, and the head groomer—a woman whom we shall call Kate—had known Sadie since she was a tiny puppy. As a result, Sadie was delighted to see Kate—and I could expect that Sadie wouldn't be traumatized by being separated from me, since she already knew all about "the grooming routine."

The first time we came into the salon, the knowledgeable Kate was able to explain to me all of the things that Sadie would need for her upkeep. Our initial meeting lasted a good half an hour while Kate covered in detail all of the various grooming issues for a Maltese. There was actually quite a lot involved in taking care of a small dog like this, or so I was starting to learn, such as that Sadie needed to have her anal sacs regularly expressed.

As with tear stains, I had never encountered this anal sac issue with my big dogs before, but apparently anal gland problems are quite common in smaller breeds of dog. The anal glands are a pair of small scent-producing glands at the base of the dog's tail. In larger dogs these glands express themselves naturally when the dog defecates, releasing a smelly fluid. However, in toy dogs the glands sometimes can become "impacted," and, if not regularly expressed, can become infected or even rupture, with terrible health consequences for the dog.

Anal gland problems account for the "scooting" behavior often seen in smaller dogs, something usually incorrectly blamed on parasites. I had been reluctant to begin probing around under Sadie's tail, as you might imagine, even though I had seen her "scooting" around a bit, and I was aware that she had some sort of discomfort happening back there. As with eye stains, though, I had little idea what to do about it.

I was delighted to learn that for a small extra fee Kate would be happy to express Sadie's anal glands, and would clean the tear stains from around her eyes. These were both tasks I could have managed on my own—many small dog owners take care of these things themselves. However, I thought it a real boon to find a groomer who, for a small fee, would accomplish these things for me. Kate was a professional, and these chores were swiftly completed without distress on the dog's part, whereas I would have labored over them, and probably inflicted discomfort if not pain upon my little friend. I remember feeling extremely grateful to Kate—the extra five dollars I was paying for these services seemed eminently reasonable.

The last thing on Kate's agenda that day was to discuss what kind of hairstyle Sadie should have. I had originally thought that I could just brush Sadie's coat myself, and leave it at that. She was a tiny dog. How hard could she be to brush? But I was now learning that Sadie's coat was going to require more upkeep than I had imagined.

Maltese coats, it turns out, are more like hair than fur. Maltese are actually considered a "non-shedding" breed because they have a minimal undercoat and as a result don't shed much—so they make good pets for people with allergies. However, they also have been bred for long show-coats, and they have hair-like topcoats that constantly grow out, just the way human hair constantly grows out. These topcoats need either to be combed and bound up to keep them from tangling, or the dogs need to be given regular haircuts, the same way humans need haircuts.

In Sadie's case, since we were always out with Willow at conservation areas, I thought that it would be impractical to let her grow out a long showy coat—especially since I hoped that eventually she would be down on the ground walking with Willow. So on Kate's advice, we opted for a shorter 'do'.

There are actually a number of different short haircuts that are used on Maltese, Bichons, Coton de Tulear, Toy Poodles, and other such small furry dog breeds, depending upon the dog's coat texture and length. Many of the cuts have been devised for the show ring, and are quite exaggerated, such as the Lion Cut, where the dog's butt is shaved and a large ruff of fur left around its neck. I looked at a lot of photographs in the grooming salon's notebook of different hairstyles, including the Lamb Cut and the Teddy Bear Cut, but we decided that a "Puppy Cut" would look the cutest and most natural on Sadie.

Kate explained the Puppy Cut to us: She would neatly trim short the fur on Sadie's face, including her little moustache and beard. Then the coat covering her body would all be trimmed to one length using a trimmer with a 5/8 inch blade. Of course, at first, most of Sadie's hair was shorter than this—though eventually she would grow out a thick, tousled topcoat that we would let grow to two to three inches long before hacking it back.

"Okay," Kate said. "I think that's everything." She paused to look at me. Then she said, "You have to leave now."

During our entire conference, I had been holding Sadie tightly to my chest, probably in unconscious anticipation of the moment when I would be expected to part with her to be groomed. Keep in mind, I had been carrying this little dog around with me like a baby for several weeks, and I was terrified of handing her over to anyone else, even Kate. I found myself stalling for time.

I needed reassurance about Sadie's toenails, which Kate had already promised to trim. The one time I had tried trimming Sadie's tiny black toenails myself, with a nail clipper, I drew a gusher of blood. I feared this tiny creature would bleed to death before the blood would stop, and I rushed her to a vet who applied a styptic pencil, and advised me to always keep one on hand if I was going to cut my dog's nails.

Kate explained to me that I had been using the wrong equipment. Instead of a nail clipper, she used a dremel on smaller dogs, which is a device about the size of an electric screwdriver. She took one out to show me. The dremel consisted of a bit of sandpaper on a rotating mount that would grind down the nails rather than cutting them off. The nails of tiny dogs are prone to breakage, apparently, and since Sadie's nails were black it was hard to see where the quick was—so there was always the risk of disaster in cutting them. Using the dremel was a much kinder and safer procedure, especially in the hands of someone like Kate, who knew what she was doing.

I had by now exhausted even Kate's patience.

"Okay, momma," she said. "Let's have the baby." She leaned over and took Sadie from my arms, and shoved me less than gently out the door of the salon.

I'm sure that I looked as worried as a young mother leaving her child at preschool for the first time. I drove around frantically for two hours, circling the groomer's location and waiting to get my dog back. I had made Kate promise that this first grooming would be done in two hours. *No more than two hours!*

I'm sure that I called the salon at least three times during this period to see how Sadie was doing. They must have thought I was crazy. At last I got a call on my cell phone that my dog was done, and I rushed back, and stormed in the door expecting the worst, fearing in fact some kind of trauma.

When I came in the door of the salon, Kate had Sadie waiting for me, perched serenely atop the checkout desk. I barely recognized her. Was this Sadie? She had gone from brownish off-white to a gleaming pure snow white. Her tear stains and crusts were completely erased, nails trimmed, glands expressed, and a new pink kerchief knotted about her neck. She was gorgeous!

"Oh my god!" I cried to Kate, as she handed me back this brilliantly white and sweet-smelling lapdog—who was wriggling with excitement to see me. "She looks like a new dog! What did you do with my old dog?"

Sadie looked like a real Maltese now. Her bright white coat contrasted nicely with her black shoe-button eyes and black nose, and with the pink wisp of tongue poking out of her mouth—which itself matched the kerchief. The groomers had even gone so far as to polish her few remaining teeth.

Kate laughed at my reaction and agreed that Sadie "cleaned up well," and she scolded me a little that I hadn't brought her in sooner. Of course, Kate couldn't know the kind of shape Sadie had been in when we first got her. And now you would never have known it. Sadie was rapidly turning back into the little white princess I had met at the bus stop on Calista's arm three years earlier. This shouldn't have surprised me, I suppose, but at the time Sadie's transformation seemed nothing short of miraculous.

I should say here that, while Kate couldn't have known exactly how badly Sadie had been neglected, she clearly had heard something. Marshfield wasn't that big of a town. And it turned out that Kate was also still grooming Bandit. So she knew that both dogs had gone to new homes after Calista's death. And now, having spoken with both adoptive families and seen both dogs, Kate apparently had some idea of what had transpired.

Kate also seemed to know Bob Piero, having groomed both dogs since they were puppies. Before I left the salon, I asked Kate, "How is Bandit doing? Did he land in a good place?"

Kate assured me that Bandit had a great new family, and kids to play with, and that he was doing well.

"You don't think the Pieros are going to want them back, do you?" I asked her, meaning the dogs. I hadn't heard a peep from the family since we'd gotten Sadie from them, but Dan had been pestering me with questions about whether or not we could keep Sadie. We were all getting more attached to her, and the same question had been niggling at the back of my own mind.

"Well, now, that wouldn't really be fair to you, would it?" Kate said, a bit severely. "Not after you spent all that time and money fixing her up."

This was not the reassurance I was hoping for. "No," I agreed. "But I'd feel bad if the Piero kids wanted her back. It would be hard to say no to them, wouldn't it?"

"If they want her back," Kate advised, "Tell them you want to be reimbursed for the vet and grooming bills. Bob Piero will never do it."

I sighed. Another woman who didn't like Bob Piero. I wondered if he'd stiffed Kate on her bills, the way she was talking, and if that was why he'd stopped having the dogs groomed.

This conversation had done nothing to put my mind at ease. I certainly didn't want to be fighting the Pieros for custody of Sadie.

It also crossed my mind for the first time that Bob Piero might be using me as a free and very convenient dog sitter, someone to pay the vet and grooming bills and to take care of the dog until he and his kids could get settled in their new home. That possibility hadn't even entered my mind previously. Though it seemed unlikely, the suggestion made me feel vulnerable and slightly sick—as I collected my newly clean, perfumed, and glisteningly white lapdog, and took her home with me.

Chapter 8

MINI ME

Now that Sadie was cleaned up, I was starting to get a much better look at her—and I began to be very curious about where she had come from. Even in her somewhat diminished state, she was still an adorable little dog, especially after her bath. She was starting to look to me like a regular little show dog. However, once I had her up on my kitchen counter, and was regularly putting medications down her throat and touching up her tear stains, I began to notice that she had a rather funny shape.

She was a bit jacked-up in the rear, sort of like a little race car. Either her front legs were slightly too short, or her back legs were slightly too long, I could never tell which. She also had one "wall eye." When you looked at her straight on, one of her eyes had a narrow white streak that ran around the upper inside of one corner and down the side of her eye, and this marred what otherwise would have been a perfect pair of black shoe-button eyes. If you compared her with pictures of real Maltese show dogs, you could see that Sadie actually did not have very good conformation by breed standards. Plainly this was no highly-bred specimen of a Maltese dog, and I began to wonder where Calista had gotten her.

We had located Sadie's original vet—the doctor who had taken care of her when she was a puppy—in order to obtain her medical records. In the course of talking to this vet, we were told that Sadie had come from a pet shop at one of our local malls. This fact was confirmed by the bus stop mothers, who even managed to get me a phone number for the store.

By the time I called, however, the number had been disconnected and the pet store appeared to have gone out of business. Apparently it was some kind of franchise for a chain of pet stores, and they had relocated. Still, this was valuable information. It meant that Sadie had probably been supplied by a distributor for the chain, and almost certainly had come from a so-called "puppy mill," one of those commercial dog breeding operations that supply puppies to chain stores and online retailers.

Given our location in Boston, this also likely meant that Sadie had likely come from a puppy mill in Pennsylvania—which at the time was home to the largest number of commercial dog breeders in the northeastern United States. This made perfect sense to me—and it explained a lot. It certainly explained why Sadie was no beauty queen.

Puppy mill breeders, I knew, wanted dogs that looked cute and like specific AKC breeds, but they were not show breeders, and they could be assumed to have little or no interest in the finer points of conformation. Rumors abounded back then that puppy mills often bred from AKC castoffs or "culls." Some suggested that this meant puppy mill puppies were more likely to have genetic and physical defects than were dogs from so-called "reputable" AKC breeders, and perhaps this was the case.

However, having already had genetic problems with a purebred collie from a so-called "reputable" breeder—overly close breeding appeared to be the source of Willow's arthritis problems—I must confess that I was more than a bit skeptical of the claim that "reputable" conformation breeders were "better." My own experience had been that conformation breeders often breed their stock far too closely in order to achieve the fashionable styles and coats they want for the show ring.

Say what you want about commercial breeders. The thing you can be sure of is that they seek—more than anything—to breed tough indestructible dogs that are able to survive the agricultural conditions in which they are raised, and the subsequent shipping and handling by distributors and retailers. Dogs with genetic or health problems are almost certainly "culled" or euthanized, and unlike show breeder castoffs, are not generally foisted off upon an unknowing public as "pet quality" puppies—as they are euphemistically termed.

This is not to argue in favor of "puppy mills." Over the years commercial dog breeding operations have acquired their own well-deserved bad reputations based upon their industrial style treatment of man's best friend. I will not belabor here the conditions under which puppy mill dogs are raised—others have already done that. Suffice to say that commercial dog breeding operations are similar to other kinds of livestock breeding businesses, such as those through which chicken, pigs and sheep are raised. The breed stock used in such operations are usually confined to small crates or boxes, and the animals often spend most of their lives in these cramped conditions, with little or no room to move around or stretch their legs. There is generally no outdoor play, or human kindness.

The Pennsylvania puppy mills were especially notorious in the early aughts for their poor treatment of their animals, though I should add here that I have no direct evidence that this is where Sadie came from. If you have a strong stomach, there are videos of the worst of these commercial pet-rearing operations on YouTube. Lancaster, PA, has historically had the highest concentration of puppy mills of any county in the nation, and has been dubbed the "Puppy Mill Capital of the East."

The puppies produced by these commercial dog-raising businesses were usually taken from their mothers at very young ages, when they were just weaned, were administered the few shots mandated by law, and then were crated and whisked off to distributors and to pet stores for display—where they might languish for weeks if they were not lucky enough to be quickly sold. Little thought was generally given to the socialization of puppies at the very time when they should have been learning to play well with others. This often resulted in poorly socialized, frightened or aggressive adult dogs.[1]

---

[1] I am speaking here about the early aughts. It should be noted that, since that time, the USDA and the AKC have both made efforts to inspect commercial dog breeding operations, and to crack down upon the worst of the "puppy mills." So the situation with commercial dog breeding may have improved somewhat. However, the AKC has also, in recent years, begun registering purebred dogs produced by large agricultural breeders, and in some instances has worked to block animal welfare legislation. So what constitutes a "reputable breeder" today is less than clear, and an AKC registration certificate no longer is any guarantee that a dog did not come from a puppy mill.

If Sadie was in fact a puppy mill dog, as I believe she was, then this would certainly explain her lack of socialization, and the way she was behaving towards Willow. This background would also account for her general scrappiness and will to live. Her puppy mill breeding almost guaranteed that she would not be an easy dog to kill, no matter how badly she was treated. A sensitive, highly-bred show dog like Willow would probably not have survived what Sadie had been through. Sadie, though, given the tiniest sliver of a chance, would thrive.

As a result of my encounter with Sadie, I have come to have a great admiration for puppy mill dogs. For how tough and determined they are, and what they can endure. I certainly wouldn't recommend getting a commercially raised dog from a pet store chain or online retailer due to the significant socialization problems that can occur with such dogs. However, I do suspect that agriculturally-bred dogs are probably hardier and more resilient than are the highly bred show dogs produced by so-called "reputable" conformation breeders—if for no other reason than by virtue of having survived such "Darwinian conditions."

Lest I come off as heartless, and as a promoter of puppy mills, let me also say that—once I had looked into agricultural dog raising operations and become convinced that Sadie was almost surely one of these commercially-bred dogs—I couldn't help but picture what her young life must have been like. It isn't a stretch to imagine that she was probably born with five or six other tiny Maltese puppies, no bigger than gerbils, into one of those tight breeding crates, with barely enough room for her mother to turn around.

Sadie's mother, who probably looked a lot like Sadie herself, had surely birthed litter after litter, and was doing her doggie best to raise Sadie and her other wee puppies in these confined conditions. She would have had little or no human attention except for occasional feedings and the administration of meds. My heart breaks when I imagine Sadie's poor little Maltese mom, living out her life in that cramped birthing box, without ever being able to go outside for a walk. There would have been, for her, only month after month of breeding and bearing and nursing, until she reached the age of four or five, when she would no longer have been useful as breeding stock and would probably have been summarily euthanized.

The life of Sadie's mother is almost unbearable to think about for anyone who has ever loved one of these tiny lapdogs. But her daughter Sadie, well, she was making up for lost time. If ever there was a survivor, and a dog that drew people in to care for her, it was certainly our little Sadie.

With Sadie feeling better, and gaining back her fur and strength, she was suddenly showing an interest in getting down to walk with Willow on our expeditions out—rather than only riding around inside my shirt or jacket. This was something of a relief since it was now high summer and it was getting a bit hot and sweaty in there. The weather was beautiful, and both dogs seemed to want to be out and about.

I didn't want to put a collar and leash on Sadie, since I couldn't imagine tugging her around by her scrawny little neck. And so I got her a soft vest with Velcro closures to wear around outside. I also got a retractable leash that connected to a steel loop at the back of the vest so she could move about freely. The vest, which looked like a small pink life jacket on her, gently restrained her increasingly vigorous little body.

At first Willow wasn't wild about having Sadie out walking with us—to say nothing of down on the ground with him—and he tried mostly to avoid her. She had been so snappy and disagreeable towards him in the house that you could hardly blame the poor fellow. I felt sorry for even bringing Sadie along, and for allowing her to run around on a leash beside him.

I had kept waiting for things between the two dogs to improve. That is the advice you always hear about dogs in the same house. "Just let them work it out," people say. But Willow and Sadie had not worked anything out. Not only was Sadie still snapping at my mild-mannered collie, and attacking him whenever he tried to move about the house, she was also disturbing his rest.

The moment Willow would settle down for a nap on his dog bed in the foyer, or on one of the carpets in the house, Sadie would seize the opportunity to try and nap on top of him, just the way she used to nap atop Bandit. However, unlike Bandit, Willow was not prepared to gracefully accept this indignity. The moment Sadie would try and climb on his back, he would leap to his feet and shake her off—not an easy thing for an arthritic dog to do. I had seen Willow snap at Sadie a few times, and feared he might actually bite her.

As Sadie tried to climb on Willow repeatedly, you could almost hear him shouting at her—as he clambered to his feet yet again— "What the heck are you trying to do?!"

Once Sadie had gone flying off Willow's back a few dozen times, she finally curled up on his fluffy tail instead, and went to sleep smack up against his furry butt, hugging against him—for warmth, I assumed. I was quite sure that Willow hated this as well, since he often still tried to snap at Sadie, but having her on his tail must have been better than having her on his back—for it wasn't enough to make him leap up and stress his painful knees.

The humiliation, though, did not end there. When it was time for us to go out for our walks, Sadie would race around Willow's prone form and would bite and pull at his fur, trying to get him up, since with his sore knees he was slow to rise. Sometimes in her excitement, she would grasp Willow's head with her front legs and begin "humping" his head.

Yes, Sadie would literally grab poor Willow by his long collie nose and start humping away with her little hips.

I had never seen a female dog go around humping other dogs before, though this was plainly what Sadie was up to. I'm told that female dogs sometimes do this as a gesture of dominance. What made this situation even more bizarre, though, was the size disparity between the two dogs.

"That is the strangest thing I have ever witnessed," Steve remarked, when he saw Sadie do this "humping" activity on Willow's face for the first time. "I don't know why he doesn't flatten her. He's like forty times her size."

"I know," I said, shaking my head despairingly. "He must think she's the boss, or something."

Of course, Willow knew very well that he would be punished—by us—if he did flatten tiny Sadie, or if he actually tried to bite her. So we weren't helping the poor fellow out much by feigning to "ignore the situation." Poor Willow, I thought. He couldn't win.

Fortunately, an unexpected degree of relief arrived the moment we were all out walking together, and with Sadie down on the ground. Sadie had clearly never done much walking outside before, something she was starting to appear well capable of doing. Now that she had her strength back, she was proving a downright peppy walker, zipping about at the end of her long retractable lead. And she was very curious about everything— wanting to rush forward and smell things, and explore.

The funny thing was that—never having been treated as a "real dog" before—Sadie had very little idea of what she was supposed to do, now that she was down on the ground and accompanying us to the places where we usually went— out to the point on the river, or to the various conservation areas near us. In her previous life, Sadie apparently had been a doll, a plaything, a toy. Nobody had ever walked her very much, and she rarely got outside, other than perhaps when she escaped with Bandit. And so she began on our walks to follow Willow around, and to imitate everything he did. Absolutely everything.

If Willow started to smell a bush while we were out, she would immediately rush over and smell it, too. If he stopped to "spray" something—a rock or a tree, as male dogs will do—she would do her best to do exactly the same. She was apparently learning how to be a "real dog" for the first time, by following Willow around and doing everything he did, exactly as he did it.

At first Willow treated Sadie with the irritation and contempt that you might expect from a large male dog being followed around by his "kid sister." Initially he tried simply to get away from her. And then, when that proved impossible, with her always scampering underfoot, he seemed to resign himself to his new job of "showing Sadie how to be a dog." You could almost see him wagging his head at how utterly clueless she was.

I have to say something here about Sadie's attempts to urinate like a male dog because they were so utterly ludicrous.

At first Sadie would watch Willow cock his leg, and then would try to do the same, sticking her own rear leg out to the side. However, she could never quite get the hang of actually bending or cocking her rear leg like a male dog. And so she would simply extend her own rear leg out to the side for a moment, leg straight, toe pointed like a ballet dancer. And then she would put her leg down again, and pee in a squat like any female dog ordinarily would.

This solution seemed not to please her, however, for she kept modifying her efforts. For a while she would actually lift off the ground with both rear feet, so that she was performing a little handstand. I have no idea whether or not she actually managed to squeeze out any drops of urine in this bizarre position, but it couldn't have been very comfortable for her. I, of course, was trapped in paroxysms of laughter watching this tiny white lapdog doing handstands and trying to "wipe down" the very same branches as her big collie brother, most of these "targets" well above her head.

In the end, Sadie learned to squat to pee while keeping one rear leg lifted off to the side. This seemed to satisfy her, and it was how she would urinate from then on. She never did quite master the fine art of cocking her rear leg like a male dog, but at least she had arrived at a more comfortable posture in which to do her business.

And Willow—though he never seemed particularly happy to be followed everywhere by his little white shadow—had regained his position as the "top dog"—at least outside of the house.

Even inside the house, things were much better between the two dogs. Sadie was finally more deferential towards Willow and stopped trying to climb on his back. He began to permit her to nap on his fluffy tail without snapping at her. However, Sadie would still misbehave whenever she got overly excited about going out, and would still bite Willow's fur and try to hump his head. But these efforts on her part now seemed more playful than dominant, and Willow started controlling the situation by pushing her over with his long nose, less than gently, and forcing her onto her back, and holding her there. Sadie would then lie in a submissive posture while he smelled her privates, as adult dogs will often do with puppies.

Of course, the moment Willow let Sadie back up again, she would be right back to humping his nose. She was irrepressible that way—wild, determined, impossible to control. Willow often still wanted to retreat to his tie-out in the front yard, to get away from her.

After a time, the two dogs got to be rather like an old married couple—The vivacious Sadie was like the young wife, always after Willow to be more active and to go out and do things. While Willow, the arthritic gentleman, preferred to be left alone on his tie-out under the big pine tree in the front yard, and to keep an eye on the cars and people and other dogs coming down our street.

Mini Me

Still, when I would come home after a long day out, they would always be sleeping together, Sadie curled up on Willow's fuzzy tail, Willow placidly asleep. When I came in, the two dogs would lift their heads in unison to see who it was. There would be one dog head lifting at either end of Willow's big furry body.

Dan and I laughed about this, and referred to them as "the two-headed dog" or the "push-me-pull-you." That's what it looked like to us. Willow looked like the push-me-pull-you from Doctor Doolittle, with a head at either end of his big hairy body, one big head big and one little head, both gazing at us.

Chapter 9

TESSA

One afternoon, while Dan and Willow were away playing with friends, there came a tapping at the front door. When I went to answer it, I saw—through the small panes in the wooden door—Tessa Piero's distinctive angular face and light blue-green eyes, staring back at me. She was flanked by two other girls from our neighborhood, both sunburned blonds of nine or ten years old, one of whom I recognized as Peggy Marsten's daughter. The other was a chubby girl who I knew lived farther out on the point.

My heart sank. I hadn't heard anything from the Pieros in weeks, and after our stint at the groomers I had decided that I was just being paranoid about "being used" by Bob Piero. Over time, my worries had subsided that the Piero kids would try and reclaim Sadie. But now here was Tessa Piero, standing on my doorstep with her two friends.

Reluctantly, I swung open the door, and did my best to smile at this small gang of prepubescent girls. "Hi kids," I said, with more heartiness than I felt. "What can I do for you today?"

Tessa didn't smile back at me. "We're here to take Sadie out," she said. Her tone was respectful, but determined. I would even go so far as to say demanding.

I must have paused in responding. But what could I say? I had promised this girl that she could visit anytime she wanted, and here she was.

It was at this moment that Sadie, who had been sleeping on the couch in the living room, must have heard Tessa's familiar voice. She came tearing out to the foyer, wriggling all over, and nearly leapt into Tessa's arms, yipping and barking.

I watched, cringing inside, while the girls fell all over my little lapdog, petting and stroking her, and while Sadie howled and cried, and generally greeted Tessa like the long lost dog-owner that she was.

It was at this juncture that the girl from the point stepped forward, and said, in a formal tone suggesting that she was carrying a message from her mother, "Tessa's just visiting for the day. We'll bring Sadie back later."

"Oh, of course," I said, feeling somewhat relieved by this. Also, what would I have said otherwise? No, you can't have her? "Let me just get her leash," I said. "Hold on a minute."

As I retrieved Sadie's little life-jacket vest and retractable leash, I thought to myself, *A visit*. A visit I could handle. *Breathe*, I told myself. *Keep breathing*. I don't think I had realized until that moment how attached I was getting to this little dog.

With Sadie's gear in my hands, I came back to the door, and strapped the tiny dog into her harness. It took me a moment to fasten the Velcro closures around her little body, which was still wiggling furiously. Then I handed the leash to Tessa.

Tessa gazed at me coldly. "We used to have nice jackets for her," she said.

There was resentment in the girl's glare. She had plainly taken Sadie's improved condition, and my putting on her harness, as some sort of pointed rebuke, though of course I didn't mean it that way. I'm sure I said something kindly-sounding like, "Of course you did," or something of that sort, when what I really wanted to say was, *It wasn't your fault*. But of course I couldn't say that either, because it would imply that Sadie's condition had been her father's fault, or her brother's fault. And so I kept silent, and waved the three girls goodbye as they tore off into the neighborhood with a tiny white lapdog bouncing delightedly at their heels.

Whatever trauma Sadie had suffered, she clearly didn't hold it against Tessa, and she obviously still adored the girl—probably much more than she would ever love me and my family, or so I thought wretchedly. Watching them go, I felt jealous and more than a little sad. I was also worried. *What if they didn't bring her back? Then what would I do?*

"Try and have her back by dinner time," I called helplessly after them. By this time, of course, they were already out of sight.

What if Tessa took Sadie home with her? That was my main concern as the minutes ticked by and as I waited for Sadie to be returned to me. I spent the next two hours trying to work in my office, and getting absolutely nothing done. I couldn't help but listen intently for the girls coming back, and jumped up at the slightest noise. I tried to calm myself with the thought that the Pieros were probably living by now in their "rental" that "didn't allow pets." Assuming any of that was true in the first place.

Finally, I couldn't take it any more. I walked as casually as I could out to the point, to the house where I knew Tessa's friend lived. It was a pretty, rose-strewn Cape on the water, and as I knocked on the door I could hear the girls' flute-like voices inside, coming from a back bedroom. The friend's mother, a sleepy looking blonde with streaky hair I knew from the bus stop, answered the door, and I spoke briefly with her. "I'm just here to check on Sadie," I said. "Is she doing okay?"

The woman laughed, and said, "Don't worry. You'll get her back."

She explained that the girls were still having their play date. Tessa was going home at five, and the girls would return the dog before she left. This woman clearly had no intention of keeping Sadie, or of allowing Tessa to take her home with her. She told me that it was "nice of me" to let the girls play with the dog.

I felt somewhat better after I had talked with this other mother. I had the definite impression that there was someone in charge here, keeping things organized. This woman presumably knew what had happened with the Pieros' dogs, and wasn't going to get all dewy-eyed about sending Sadie back to live with Tessa, no matter how devoted girl and dog were to each other.

I went back home, and sure enough, shortly before five the three girls came racing back with a now exhausted Sadie, and thrust her into my arms, before darting away again.

"We'll be back again next week!" they shouted, as they ran off. "Same day, same time!"

"Okay," I called after them, my heart sinking again. Tessa clearly wasn't giving up on her tiny Maltese dog.

That evening was a tough one at our house. Steve and Daniel were both outraged that I had let Sadie fall back into the Pieros's hands, even for one moment—even though it was just Tessa and her two friends. "It's so unfair!" Dan cried, hugging Sadie to him, nearly in tears. After part of the summer with us, Sadie was already very much a member of our family, and Daniel—though he had been there when I had told the Piero kids they could visit—absolutely refused to understand it now. Here I was, halfway to giving back his new dog, as far as he was concerned. He was furious with me.

Sadie had turned out to be the perfect companion for my young son. Dan was a bit of a nerdy kid—eschewing all sports except for karate, and preferring instead to spend his time after camp reading and drawing cartoons, and—to the extent I'd let him—playing video games. Sadie soon joined in on all of these activities, sitting on Dan's lap while he read or drew, or sharing his snacks and meals after school while he played video games or traded Pokemon cards with his friends.

After just this short period, it was as if Dan no longer remembered a time when he didn't have a little white dog in the house to accompany him in his every activity. The idea that this indispensible new friend might now be taken away was unfathomable to him. He gasped the word "unfair" at me with an incredulous and injured air that said mere words didn't begin to capture how he felt. What I was threatening to do to his world was truly beyond belief.

Steve was even worse than Dan. I had tried to explain to my husband—who hadn't been there—that I had promised the Piero kids they could visit Sadie any time, and that they could have her back in six months—only if they promised to care for her properly, of course. I wasn't going to give the dog back without some assurances on their part. Still, at the time I didn't feel I could just renege on the promises I had made, no matter how my family felt about it. And I still felt some belated obligation to Calista.

Steve, though, had made no such promises. And he had seen the condition in which Sadie had arrived at our home. That was enough for him. The little dog wasn't going back to the Pieros. Not now. Not ever. Steve was quite steadfast on this point, and never wavered.

"No way," he said. "They aren't getting her back. Forget it. They had their chance to kill her. Let them get another dog to kill."

My husband may have sounded a bit heartless about the Piero children—and it wasn't like him. Steve is usually such a big softie. To understand why, you have to understand a few things about my husband's relationship with this little dog.

When we first got Sadie, if you had asked me, I would not have said that the person in our household who would be closest to her would be Steve. Dan and I were certainly around the house more, and we seemed more natural companions for a little lapdog, mother and child. And each of us had our own daily routines with Sadie, me walking her in the mornings and evenings, and Dan playing with her in the afternoons. What I did not appreciate, though, at least at first, was the affinity of disposition and shared evening rituals of a Boston attorney and a tiny Maltese dog.

I was partly responsible for the two of them bonding so closely. I can see that now.

Once Sadie had settled into our house, I had attempted to enforce what I now look back on as "the Big Dog Rules." The dogs in my home (and I'd had several over the years) had always been expected to conform to certain standards of behavior, which included admonitions such as no rushing the front door to greet guests and no begging for food at mealtimes. Dogs were expected to go and lie down quietly while the humans ate—something Willow had been trained to do from a young age.

What I had not counted on, though, was that these rules would prove nearly impossible to apply to the irrepressible Sadie. Also, that she would have an ardent ally in my husband.

This all came out, as family disputes often do, over dinner. As Sadie shifted from being a starved waif who we were trying to revive, to a fully functioning member of the household, I began trying to apply the Big Dog Rules to her, including not mooching at meals. This ill-fated attempt on my part came—I should add—on the heels of a whole history of mealtime anarchy at our house.

I had met my husband when he was a thirty-five year old bachelor attorney living in a seaside cottage in Quincy, MA, that he was slowly renovating on the weekends. Every room in this small house was heaped with tools and books and paint. There was very little furniture of any kind. Steve had gotten into the habit each evening of reheating prepared meals or leftovers, and then collapsing on his one rickety Victorian horsehair couch in the living room in front of the television, to eat his dinner while he watched something that made him laugh. That was how Steve had always relaxed after a long day at the law office—by laughing along with Seinfeld or the Simpsons, or, later, Jon Stewart.

Steve has always been an independent and self-amusing sort, and marrying him meant not trying to turn him into someone else, or make him do things that he didn't want to do, such as a lot of socializing. I cleared out the tools and paint, and brought in some new furniture and bookshelves. But formal family dinners, with everyone reporting on their day, was clearly not in the cards. Steve's family had done that while he was growing up, and Steve had detested being forced to "sit still and eat his peas."

After Dan came along, I made a few brief stabs at enforcing family dinner times, but it was hopeless. Dan was a tremendously picky eater who was starving by five. Steve rarely got home from the office before seven or eight at night, at which point he would vacuum up Dan's leftover macaroni and cheese or chicken nuggets—food that I wouldn't eat because I was trying to get back my pre-motherhood figure. At that point I mostly wanted salads.

Eventually I just relented, and fixed everyone separate meals as meals were required. It wasn't worth the struggle trying to get everyone sitting down at the same time, and eating the same thing. We were all extremely verbal types, and not eating meals together was hardly putting a damper on the lively conversations we always had at our house. In fact, a meal alone could often be a break from trying to "get a word in edgewise," as my mother used to say.

Into this chaotic situation waltzed our little Sadie, and she immediately took up residence on Steve's lap in the evenings in front of the television, along with Steve's dinner and his evening paper. I ignored this at first because we were, as previously noted, just extremely glad to have Sadie eating again and putting on weight. However, there did come a night when Sadie was clearly no longer at risk of starving to death, and I found myself watching Steve and Sadie together in the living room as they picked over the carcass of a rotisserie chicken.

Steve would drop his paper momentarily to pluck off a piece of chicken for Sadie, and hand-feed it to her. She would carefully and meticulously eat the piece of chicken and then lick the grease from Steve's fingers. Steve would then break off his own piece of chicken, and up would go the paper. Sadie, sitting on his knees, would wait patiently for the paper to drop again. If Steve took too long to give her another bite, Sadie would start to bat at the paper, with a thumping sound, or sometimes utter a little bark or howl, to nudge him along. Eventually Steve would drop the paper again, and the whole feeding ritual would start over.

I watched all of this for a minute or two, then asked, "Isn't this a little gross?"

Steve dropped his paper, and looked at me briefly. He shrugged.

"Do you think there's any chance I could get you to eat at the table?" I asked. "Just until she's trained not to beg?"

The paper went back up.

"Steve, honey," I insisted. "That's really kind of disgusting."

Steve dropped his paper again, and leveled his gaze at me. "What?" he said.

"It's gross," I repeated. "Feeding the dog and then yourself like that. Unsanitary." I wrinkled up my nose.

"No," he protested. "Dogs have clean mouths. I read that somewhere."

"You have saliva all over your hands. Germs. Dog saliva."

The paper went back up.

"Look," I said. "Sadie's feeling better now. Can't we have the dogs out of the way at mealtimes? That's what we've always done." It was true. We had. But we'd always had big dogs before.

Slowly the paper came back down with a rattle.

Steve and Sadie were now the ones watching me for a long moment. You will have to believe me when I tell you that they were both wearing exactly the same expression on their faces, man and dog. If Sadie could have spoken, I swear she would have said something like, *Look, lady, we were having a perfectly nice time here. Why'd you have to come along and spoil things?* To Steve, I probably looked a lot like his mother, hand on hip, telling him to sit still and eat his peas.

After a very long moment of being glowered at by this pair, I could see that I was outnumbered.

"You two are going to keep doing that, no matter what I say, aren't you?" I asked.

"Yes," Steve answered agreeably.

Sadie let out an audible snort.

As you might expect, our little standoff was over. Steve wasn't going to change his habits this late in our married life. And now he had a little companion with whom to share his evening meals in front of the television. They were both extremely happy at how things had worked out, and nothing I could say was going to alter this.

Fortunately, I knew better than to try and make an issue out of it. Both Steve and Sadie appeared easy-going on the outside, but I knew that they both had very strong wills under those mild exteriors, as well as an independent streak that said they would have things their own way or not at all. They were actually a lot alike that way, Steve and Sadie, and, teamed up, they were quite formidable. And I sort of respected that.

Apparently there were going to be separate Big Dog Rules and Little Dog Rules at our house. Or, that is to say, the little dog was going to run rough-shod over the Big Dog Rules.

As was the case with Daniel, Steve could no longer imagine not having Sadie in his world—his little pal who kept him company in the evenings, and shared his meals during the most enjoyable part of his day. What I was doing—allowing Tessa Piero to visit, and suggesting that we might need to give Sadie back—was not only morally wrong in Steve's eyes—she had been such a mess when we got her—it was also something of a betrayal of our family as it had reorganized itself around this newest member of our household.

It sounds a bit silly today describing the strong feelings everyone had about this tiny lapdog. She was, after all, only a silly little dog. But Sadie seemed to have the ability to arouse strong feelings in everyone around her. And the strongest emotions, of course, were those she aroused in Tessa Piero, and in me.

After Tessa's visit, I was a wreck for the next few days. I kept hearing in my ears Sadie's shrill excited yapping over seeing her old owner. She clearly still loved Tessa, and Tessa adored her. And what haunted me most was the way Tessa had glared at me with those cold, cold eyes of hers. Oh, how that young girl hated me. I have rarely in all of my life been looked at with such anger, such venom.

I guess I had figured that if Tessa did visit, she would be grateful that I had fixed up her little Sadie and that she would be happy to see her dog in a good home. If the girl felt anything negative, I thought, then perhaps she might feel some shame or humiliation that her family had let the tiny dog fall into such terrible condition, as they had, and that as a result the dog had been taken from her and her brother.

These expectations on my part, though, turned out to be sheer fantasy. Hadn't I imagined reassuring Tessa that it wasn't her fault? And saying that her family had been going through a bad patch, and that things would get better? That her little dog was in a good place now where she was well cared-for, and loved?

But her family's treatment of Sadie, it was becoming clear, had barely registered with young Tessa—or if it had registered, it was no longer the foremost thing in her mind. What sat at the front of her brain now was that this was HER DOG, the dog she used to have leashes and harnesses for. And I—I was the big bad ogre—the mean adult who had taken HER DOG away from her.

She was Dorothy and Sadie was Toto. And I—I was the evil witch riding off on my bicycle with Sadie in my basket wearing my pointy witch's hat and cape.

The next few nights I lay bolt awake in my bed, imagining how all of this must look from Tessa's perspective. How would I have seen it at her age? For I, too, had once been a romantic young girl who loved dogs. The answer showed me exactly how deluded I had been.

What if someone had taken away my beloved Border Collie, Tippy, the dog I'd had at Tessa's age?

Oh, how I would have hated the people who took her from me! How I would have plotted to get Tippy back!

I would have made elaborate plans to escape with my dog—probably thought of running away from home, anything to get away from the awful adults scheming to steal my best friend from me. And I would have had long yearning fantasies about breaking into their house when they weren't at home, and stealing Tippy away from them. Or sneaking in late at night, and silently escaping with her while they slept. Hissing "Shhhh" to my dog, who would understand my meaning, and would tiptoe alongside me in the deathly quiet until we could squeeze out an open window into a waiting flower bed . . ..

I realized then, lying wide-eyed in my bed, that I had made a terrible mistake. I should never have invited the Piero kids to visit Sadie after we got her. I had thought it would soften the blow of losing their little dog. That they would be able to see she was happy and in a good place. And perhaps, for an adult, it might have worked out that way. But these were children. Tessa's visiting could serve only to arouse her ardor for her little dog, and inflame the pain of not being able to get her back. It would have been far kinder just to take the dog away, and have it over.

Those promises I had made the day we got Sadie—that the kids could visit, and maybe even get her back in six months—I realized now that they had been made mainly to spare my own feelings, not the children's. I had made the promises to make myself feel better about what I was doing. I was taking away the children's dog, and that was the bitter truth of it. Something I didn't want to have to face.

And now nobody's feelings were being spared. And everyone was angry with me. My son. My husband. And most of all Tessa and her brother, who surely hated me with all of their hearts. I had blown it. Big time.

And the worst of it was, I couldn't think now how to gracefully get us out of the situation I had created. Tessa had set herself up to visit weekly with her friends, whenever she had play dates. And what was I going to do? Turn the girls away? Hide Sadie on the afternoons when her former owner might be around?

Oh, it was all too much. I tried to console myself with the thought that perhaps Tessa's visit had been awkward enough that she might not want to come again. That perhaps one visit would be enough for her.

Such, of course, was not to be the case.

Chapter 10

SELF-IMAGE

Besides Tessa Piero's visits, the other problem I was having to contend with that summer was the whole issue of small dogs and self-image, which was finally starting to catch up with me. I certainly was aware by this point that carrying around a little white lapdog on your arm or tucked in your jacket might influence how people viewed you. My dog-walking group had—by this time—made that abundantly clear.

Still, by withholding the full force of their opinions, my friends had perhaps soft-pedaled the news about what Sadie was doing to the way people looked at me. It took running into a more hard-nosed friend to bring things into focus—someone who had known me in the years before motherhood. Someone who knew me professionally back in the days when I was practicing law and commuting to work daily in a black size-four silk suit and four-inch heels.

This perhaps inevitable event occurred sometime in the heat of midsummer. The circumstances were that I had reconnected with an old friend—we shall call her "Alice"—over the fact that we were both now "doing the writing thing." Although I had been in touch with Alice off and on,

Self-image

we hadn't actually seen each other in person in a few years, not since I had become a mother (Alice was married, but childless, and was still practicing law at an arts nonprofit). We were both looking forward to catching up on our lives and having a long, leisurely conversation over a good meal. We made plans to go out for dinner at a nice restaurant down in Plymouth, Massachusetts. But Alice, like most of my friends, had been hearing about my adventures adopting Sadie via email, and she wanted first to swing by my house to "see the famous Maltese herself." Alice just had to meet "this tiny hairless wretch" that had caused my family so much consternation, and to see what all the "fuss was about."

Of course, by this time, Sadie had more or less recovered and much of the "fuss" was over. I tried to dissuade Alice from coming by before we went out, mostly because I didn't want to have to clean up my house. With a middle-grade child and two dogs running around the place, our home was never all that tidy, and I wasn't looking forward to trying to pluck all of Daniel's Star Wars Legos out of the oriental carpets I had inherited from my mother. Still, Alice would not be deterred, and insisted upon meeting Sadie, saying, "Don't you just love these teeny, tiny dogs?!"

Interestingly, Alice was not herself a dog owner, due to her severe allergies, she claimed. Still her overheated excitement at my tales of Sadie's rescue suggested to me that Alice was herself playing with the idea of getting a little lapdog, something she admitted when I saw her—preferably a "non-shedding breed," she explained, so that her allergies "wouldn't be so much of a concern." Alice was a thin, austere, artsy sort of person, and was very alert to style. And so I surmised that she, too, had been caught up in the fervor for small dogs that was increasingly in the air in those days. A fantasy must have flitted through my mind of showing off my newly white and fluffy Sadie on my arm as I greeted Alice at the door, perhaps holding it over my old friend that I now had a trendy, stylish little dog myself.

At the appointed hour, the doorbell rang, and Sadie—as she had been doing lately, now that she was feeling better—rushed the front door, giving me no opportunity to pick her up. And, reacting to the presence of what to her smelled like "a stranger," she commenced a shrill racket of barking and yapping. I followed upon my little dog's heels, and swung open the front door for my friend. As the door yawned wide, I saw Alice standing there, her fingers stuffed in her ears, gazing down with abject distaste at my shrilly yipping half-pint, who by this time was jumping up against her knees with great exuberance and enthusiasm.

"Well, this certainly is a change for you," Alice cried over the noise, appearing to wince in pain.

"Sorry," I called back. "She gets kind of excited when people she doesn't know come over." Then I did what any small dog owner does in these situations. I scooped Sadie up and wedged her under my arm—not to show her off now, but to regain control of her. This, in my opinion, is one of the reasons that small dog owners often ignore the bad behavior of their tiny charges. Small lapdogs are actually rather easy to squelch because there's not much they can do with all four feet off the ground.

Except, of course, for making noise. A lot of noise.

"Come on in," I shouted to Alice over Sadie's screeching. "She'll be quiet once we both sit down."

Self-image

Alice followed me into the living room, tripping over Dan's Legos as she went, and still holding her fingers securely in her ears.

Sadie fortunately did settle quietly into my lap once we were all sitting on the couch.

"Thank goodness!" Alice exclaimed. "My God. How do you stand it?!"

"Stand what?" I asked innocently. I was trying to be a little funny, but the truth was that by now I was rather used to Sadie's screechy little-dog barking, and it no longer bothered me—though I could well remember being offended by the noise of yapping lapdogs before I had one myself.

I think that, by that point in my life, I had gotten fairly immune to noise, as a lot of parents do. Daniel and his friends often made far more of a racket than Sadie ever did, and I had gotten pretty good at mentally shutting out the din that often surrounded me. Alice, though, being both childless and dogless, was probably justifiably appalled. Sadie's barking, when she was excited, took on a shrill, rasping quality that sounded like a metal paint scraper on wallboard. "The little paint-peeler," my friend Melissa teasingly called her.

"Seriously," Alice continued. "I've been thinking that I might like to get a small dog myself, but I truly couldn't stomach that noise. Honestly, it would kill me."

"But she's so cute," I said, stroking Sadie's soft white fur. I felt the warm slide of her pink tongue across the back of my hand. "And you sort of get used to it."

Just then we heard the sound of a key in the front door. *Uh oh.*

This, I knew, was Steve arriving home from work to cover for me watching Daniel while I went out—and he was absolutely Sadie's favorite person in the world.

The tiny dog launched herself off my lap and scrambled for the front door again, now screeching and yapping even louder than before at the sound of Steve's distinctive step. She could hardly have been more excited, and was starting to do her anticipatory dinner dance, while she waited for the entrance of the fellow who fed her off his plate every night.

"Oh my God, I can't stand it!" Alice cried. She had her fingers stuffed deeply in her ears again, and—as if reacting to an actual stab of physical pain—leapt up off the couch and raced for the door. She nearly knocked down my husband in her haste to get past him, and escape, while yelling over her shoulder at me, "I'll meet you outside, by the car!"

Surprised by Alice's sudden and swift departure, my husband and I watched her flee. Then I leaned down and scooped Sadie up under my arm, wriggling.

"Is everything okay?" Steve asked, still gazing after my friend with a bewildered look on his face.

"It's the noise," I explained. "Alice is very sensitive." I handed Sadie over to my husband. "She was being awfully loud."

Steve shrugged. He tucked Sadie under his own arm along with his evening paper, and crooned at his little friend, as if to repair some damage that had been done to her, "Shall we go and see about dinner, you poor thing?"

"Yow-yow!" Sadie replied with great delight, licking at his face.

"I thought so," said Steve. "You were just hungry, that's all. Let's go see what momma got at the grocery store today,

Self-image

shall we? There's a good dog." And off they went together, man and beast, perfectly contented in their shared evening ritual. I, for my part, went out to dinner with Alice, and tried to explain myself, and my family.

Alice was not amused, and complained all through dinner that her ears were still throbbing, and how did I possibly put up with that horrible screeching sound on a regular basis? Couldn't you have her vocal cords cut, or something? I mean, couldn't something *be done*?

When we parted ways at the end of the evening, my sensitive friend put her hand upon my sleeve. "You know," she said, "I see now that I could never have a little dog like that. There's another thing about them, besides the noise, I mean. Something you ought to know." Here Alice hesitated before leaning in confidentially, and continuing. "It's good you're giving her away," she half-whispered. "Because Sadie . . .," another hesitation, "she makes you look, well, middle-aged. You aren't going to keep her, are you? Didn't you say you were going to fix her up, and give her away?"

"Sadie makes me look middle-aged?" I asked. "Really?" I laughed out loud. Alice had to be kidding.

But no, Alice was not kidding.

"I'm perfectly serious," she said. "Not good for your image. Not good at all."

My image? Wait, what?

At first it was hard to credit much of what Alice said that evening. She was so over the top in her artsy sensitivity, and I was now remembering why we had fallen out of touch. Still, her words did sting a bit, and seemed to follow me around over the next few days. I found myself arguing in my head with her as I tried to chalk up her negative reaction to the racket Sadie had made rushing the door. Still, there was that "image" comment. *Not good for your image. Not good at all.*

Was this just Alice worrying about her own image, I wondered. Since Alice was still practicing law, she was being very careful to manage her own youthful appearance so that she didn't prematurely hit the "glass ceiling," as they called it.

Still, there was that other compound word: *Middle-aged. The dog is making you look middle-aged.*

That hurt. It was the first time I had heard that unfortunate term applied to myself, and it wasn't a pleasant experience. *And what did this all have to do with Sadie?* I couldn't help but protest in my mind that Sadie was so small and cute. How could she not *enhance* my image? And what about all those starlets who toted tiny lapdogs around in designer handbags these days? Didn't they do it to *improve* their images? Why wasn't Sadie improving mine?

I wanted to ask Steve, but I realized that this was something you couldn't ask your spouse. It was like asking, *Do these pants make me look fat?*

Does this dog make me look middle-aged?

And so I stewed. I recall asking a couple of women friends about what Alice had said, and they told me, in so many words, that I was crazy, and just to ignore her. Alice was just jealous, they said. She wanted a little dog of her own. She was overly sensitive. She was a "type." Don't listen to her.

I didn't believe them.

Alice's comments were starting to make me recall Mrs. LeBlanc and her tiny Pomeranian from next door when I was growing up. How my mother and I had reviled that

Self-image

middle-aged mom (who was probably around the age I was now, in her late thirties or early forties) with her blaring TV, her shapeless housedresses, her clouds of cigarette smoke . . . and, of course, her screechy little dog . . ..

Was that what Alice was seeing in me?

Was I turning into a shapeless Mrs. LeBlanc type, with my yappy little Maltese dog on my arm?

Chapter 11

PREJUDICE

There was only one way to tell, I decided. Only one way to determine if I was starting to turn into Mrs. LeBlanc. And that was to take a long, hard look myself in the full-length mirror at the back of my bedroom door. The next Saturday afternoon, I went upstairs, and closed the door to the master bedroom against intrusions, and turned on the overhead light. I gazed hard at myself in the long mirror at the back of the door. Sadie had followed me up the stairs, and she stood beside me, looking curiously up at me and trying to decide what I was doing.

Mirror, mirror, on the door, how much of my self-image should I abhor?

Sadie waved her little curly tail up over her back, as she always did when she was excited, and licked my bare foot. I picked her up, and snuggled her to me, and looked at myself in the mirror again. Then I put her back down, and looked at myself without her.

I picked Sadie up and put her down again several times in this way, comparing the two views of myself, both with the dog and without the dog.

Prejudice

Well, the ugly truth, I decided, was that Alice was onto something. There was a decided difference between me with Sadie, and me without Sadie.

Without Sadie, I looked exactly like what I was, somebody's mom in jeans and a V-neck T-shirt. I was no longer the slim little minx I had been in my late twenties when I had met Steve while practicing law. (How well I remembered that size four suit I used to wear!) But now it was sneakers, and size ten jeans, and a house in the burbs, and picking Legos out of the carpet down on my knees. No more condo in the city, and art museums and theater on the weekends.

My life had changed, and I had changed with it. I was still reasonably fit, with all the walking I did. But my body had gained a new heft and maturity, especially through the arms and torso. Normally, you wouldn't especially notice this extra bulk, for I was not hideously fat or anything. I still looked more or less like the same person I had always been, just more "motherly," I guess you would say.

Until I picked up Sadie. Then something unfortunate occurred.

I habitually held Sadie as if she were a small baby, sprawled across my arm, and calling attention to said arm, an arm which—one now noted in the mirror—was a rather bulky mother's arm. Not a girlish arm. A stout arm. An arm for ironing or making beds. Not a slender arm for holding a wrap in case it got cold at the movies.

And even worse, Sadie's tiny white feet, with their black teardrop pads, were catching and supporting themselves—I now saw—on the soft bulge that was my newly motherly belly—the belly I had acquired in the course of producing Daniel. In fact, this larger belly was, I saw, actually thrusting forward to catch and support the feet of this tiny dog, putting my larger girth on full display.

Oh Lord, I thought. Was everyone seeing this? Was Steve seeing it? Was Dan?

Of course they were, every time I picked Sadie up. Who was I fooling? It was everything I could do to keep from dropping Sadie on her round little head.

Of course, Steve and Dan, who knew me well and saw me every day, hadn't particularly reacted to this sight, or even probably especially noticed. But Alice, whom I hadn't seen in a long time, had zeroed in on my new and unflattering mom-image. An image that Sadie, in her baby-like way, appeared to emphasize. It was something for which, I am sorry to say, I would never quite forgive Alice, and I have not seen her since our ill-fated dinner together.

Still, it was now clear to me why those starlets looked so cute with their little lapdogs—It was their utter lack of body fat. With a slim lithe body, a tiny lapdog telegraphed a young woman's femininity and availability for motherhood.

With the extra body heft carried by even the average suburban mom, suddenly there you were, broadcasting the actual fact of motherhood itself—the fleshy bodies and mewing babies that went with it—a rather shocking sight in the mirror, especially if you had formerly been one of those lithe young things yourself. I realized it was probably no coincidence that those young starlets often carried their tiny dogs in designer handbags, so that their upper arms and bellies weren't placed on display as mine were when I held Sadie up before the mirror.

I looked down at Sadie, noticing how fluffy and girly she looked. With a deep sigh, I picked the little dog up again, determined to absorb the full brutal truth of my situation. I gazed at the two of us in the mirror again while Sadie attempted to lick my face. No, I decided, it was even worse than I had imagined, because Sadie wasn't a baby, she wasn't a child. She was an adorable pampered-looking little lapdog with what was becoming thick lush white fur. She telegraphed, not just motherhood, but something else. She telegraphed pampering, leisure, luxury, spoiling. The very things that my mother and I had seen in Mrs. LeBlanc and her Pomeranian aspiring to.

When I held Sadie in my arms, she broadcast these same things onto me and onto my newly ample form. I was no longer just a mother, a mom. No, I *became a certain kind of woman.* You know, *that kind of woman.*

I was no longer a hard-working lawyer turned writer sort of woman. That you couldn't see in the bedroom mirror. Rather, what you saw—what I saw—was a suburban housewife approaching middle age, a spoiled, lazy, snack-eating sort of woman, one with too much time on her hands and too little work to do. *Looking in the mirror, even I didn't like myself. How could anyone else like me?*

Heaving yet another deep sigh, I collapsed on the bed with Sadie and considered my dilemma. Should I keep this dog, if this was what she did to me? Was Alice right? Should I get rid of her?

Sadie settled beside me on the bed, and playfully bit at my hands, and I wrestled with her a little, pushing her onto her back and rubbing her little pink tummy. I felt pretty miserable even to be thinking about getting rid of this tiny lapdog to whom we had all become so devoted.

I can look back on this scene today with the distance of hindsight, and appreciate what a shock it must have been to catch sight of the older, more motherly figure that I was now becoming. Most of us, once we reach a certain age, carry around a fantasy that we are still the young person we were in our prime, in our late teens or early twenties, when we were at the very peak of our physical beauty, at the moment when we held only untested promise, and when our whole lives were still in front of us.

In a way, the entire rest of our lives seems a retreat from that moment, into something more solid and definite. Eventually we settle into specific jobs, into specific relationships, with specific spouses, children, and pets. We live in definite neighborhoods and definite homes, and our bodies age and our faces set into specific lines and contours that the rich, plump skin of youth once concealed. And no matter how accomplished we are, or what we actually do with our lives, we can never quite recapture all of that lost beauty and promise.

I think the fact of this is especially hard on women. Even if we are highly educated, as I certainly was, we often step off the career track, or "downshift" as they say, to raise our children. And it is the rare woman who is able to scratch her way back onto that fast track in middle age, and earn as much as men do, or command the same level of respect. And even if we do, even if we stay high-powered and whip thin, still we eventually lose the dewy beauty for which we were so valued in our youths. Indeed, it is quite shocking how precipitously a woman's self worth often drops after the age of thirty-five or forty.

I think that I was actually somewhat prepared for this, having thought long and hard before leaving the practice of law to care for my own son. I had quite intentionally left the law for another profession, one where I thought I would have better control over my working hours, and where I could raise my son myself. I didn't want someone else raising my child for me.

But not even liking the older-me that I saw in the mirror—of feeling *actually prejudiced* against myself as a "middle-aged woman"—now that came as a real shock to me. *That* was something I was *not* prepared for.

I think that I had always thought of myself as something of a feminist, as being fairly "pro-woman." But now that I was seeing myself as "a Mrs. LeBlanc," I was beginning to recognize that I myself had absorbed the values of the culture I lived in. And it was a culture that did not value women past a certain age. It certainly didn't value one who had gained a little weight, and was now carrying around a fluffy white lapdog on her arm. (I wondered momentarily if Sadie had figured into the demise of Bob and Calista Piero's marriage.)

I looked down at Sadie beside me on the bed. She had snuggled against me, and, since it didn't look like I was going anywhere, was falling asleep, her tiny white eyelids sliding shut across her black shoe-button eyes. I watched as her eyes slowly closed, and her small white form rolled onto its side. Her feet started to twitch with dreams. I rolled over onto my back myself, and pulled the bedspread over me. I was thinking more about my mother and Mrs. LeBlanc, back when I was a kid.

Mrs. LeBlanc had been five or ten years my mother's senior. She had four or five children, and was a fleshy older woman upon whom the unattractiveness of middle age had decidedly settled. My mother, by contrast, still seemed young and attractive, with a set of young twins (my brother and me), and she spent a lot of time entertaining my father's business associates, throwing cocktail parties and wearing cute 1960's dresses after the fashion of Jackie Kennedy. On some level, she probably abhorred the thought of ending up looking like Mrs. LeBlanc.

The painful thing for me, of course, was that I had not even detected the prejudices that we had all applied to Mrs. LeBlanc. Attitudes having to do with age, gender and class. But, of course, I was now the woman with the yappy little dog, and if I had not recognized the prejudices directed at Mrs. LeBlanc, I certainly detected them now, when they were being directed at me.

I saw what a sheltered life I had lived. As a young, privileged (if rural), and Ivy League-educated woman, I had traveled through life relatively unscathed by such judgments. Indeed, I was probably somewhat unsympathetic to anyone claiming to be affected by such attitudes. I was now learning a hard lesson—and one we all learn sooner or later—for nobody stays young and beautiful forever. At some point we all feel the obliterating weight of prejudice coming to rest upon us, and sense the way others are looking at us. Often, we can even see it ourselves.

When I picked up Sadie, what I saw in the mirror were the assumptions that our culture makes about women over a certain age. Assumptions that *I could see with my own prejudiced eyes.* My challenge since that time has been to understand the depth of this cultural prejudice, and to still find a way to love that woman in the mirror and the little dog beside her.

I must have reached some sort of internal arrangement with myself, for I did not immediately begin looking for

Prejudice

another home for Sadie. I wasn't going to give up on the little dog we had rescued, no matter how uncomfortable I might feel at times about "how she looked on me" or how much damage she did to my self-image—though I did of course make the usual resolutions about losing weight and working out—resolutions that I have kept with varying degrees of success since that day.

I think what has made me feel better over time, has been running into a lot of other small dog owners. Once I was regularly escorting Sadie around at the end of her leash, we immediately began meeting a whole assortment of other small dogs and their people. The dogs ranged from Chihuahuas and Jack Russell terriers, to Malti-poos and Shih tzus. Now that I had a small dog myself, these tiny lapdogs seemed—even more than before—to be everywhere, and it quickly became apparent that I had been, without knowing it, inducted into the "Club of the Small Dog."

I quickly got to know people of all ages who loved their tiny lapdogs. Many of these folks had "downsized" from bigger breeds to smaller companion dogs that they felt they could more easily handle, or that better fit with their lifestyles. Smaller dogs simply made more sense for a lot of people. Having always had large dogs myself, this was news to me. But I could now see that smaller breeds of dogs worked a lot better, especially if you lived in an apartment or condo, or in an urban area, or if you were older and didn't want the physically demanding care of a larger dog.

The funny thing was that, almost to a man and a woman, these small dog owners had noticed the same thing that I had—namely, "what a small dog did to your image." And they nearly all remarked upon it, and clearly felt rather sheepish about the whole thing. Apparently toting around a little lapdog on your arm removed whatever gravitas you might formerly have possessed, and planted you firmly amongst ranks of the frivolous and the silly.

The men seemed especially sensitive to this fact. Yes, there were a lot of men who had smaller dogs as it turned out—and they often seemed to feel quite ridiculous cuddling their little tykes. But they, like my husband, often appeared fully as devoted to their tiny charges as the women were. These men often found themselves delegated the responsibility in their families of walking their tiny canine "out in public," a somewhat humiliating exercise for them.

One fellow even confided in me, "Well, at least the neighbors usually assume that I have some frou-frou wife at home, whose dog it really is. I'd be embarrassed for people to know that this is really *my dog*. Even though *it is* my dog!" And he laughed heartily, his cheeks turning rosy with this revelation.

Lest you think that I'm making too much of this small dog and self-image thing, there's a post-script to this story that will illustrate the sorts of prejudices I now encountered. Not long after Alice's visit, I was driving through the center of our town, with Sadie on my lap, and talking into my cell phone. I came to a four-way stop, and drew to a halt. I was probably a bit distracted, since I was on the phone, but I was definitely driving slowly and carefully, as I always try to do. Still, I ended up having one of those prolonged—*You go first, No, you go first*—moments that you sometimes have at four-way stops. The guy who was headed in the other direction from me, and with whom I had this brief interaction,

Prejudice

appeared irritated as he peeled away from the intersection. Apparently I had slowed him down, and he was in a hurry.

A few days later, a letter to the editor appeared in our local paper. It was from a gentleman, and contained a long rant about *These women with their little dogs*. The letter related a story about being "trapped" at the four-way intersection in town. The man went on a long screed about small dogs and attention to the road. *Look, lady,* the letter finished, *Put down the cell phone, get the little dog off your lap, and drive!*

I have to admit, I cringed. I was pretty sure I knew who the guy was. And that he had seen the same woman I had seen in my bedroom mirror.

Chapter 12

"THE CALL OF THE SMALL"

As I found myself immersed more and more in small dog culture, I was struck by how staunchly attached and loyal people of all stripes were becoming to these tiny lapdogs. It wasn't just Paris Hilton, Britney Spears, and a bevy of little girls anymore, it was grown men and women like my husband and me.

I began to think of this increasing fondness for tiny dogs as "The Call of the Small," after Jack London's *The Call of the Wild*, one of the great dog stories of all time—though one that glorified the wildness of big dogs, not small ones. London though, it seemed to me, had it all wrong. It was, it occurred to me now, the small dogs who were really magnetic, and who actually drew us into the wild and instinctive ways of the dog. And I began to wonder why that was.

Part of it, of course, had to be simply the sheer intimacy of small dogs. I needed only to watch Daniel sprawled on the couch with Sadie to see this—while he played video games, or traded Pokemon cards with his friends. Sadie would take turns sitting on the laps of each of the boys in turn, smelling them, licking them, investigating their snacks. Or, I would observe Sadie "help" Steve with his dinner in the evenings. She was always *on you*, I thought, the moment you sat down on the couch. Life with her was so different than it was with a big dog like Willow.

In the evenings, Willow would usually go off and fall asleep on a rug somewhere. This was partly our fault, of course. As much as we loved our huge fluffy collie, a big dog like him couldn't be allowed up on the furniture, or permitted to beg for food at the table or in the living room, since his long nose could easily reach whatever you were eating. As I've said, we had quickly established Big Dog Rules and Small Dog Rules at our house. And those rules necessarily separated us from our bigger dog.

But it wasn't just the increased physical proximity of tiny lapdogs, not only that. In addition to being more physically intimate with us, Sadie also seemed to bring us into closer contact with the weird primitive ways of the canine.

I remember Steve finding me early one morning, drinking my coffee in the living room. I had my head back, and my eyes closed, and Sadie had gotten down and was carefully and thoroughly washing my feet with her long pink tongue. Normally my feet are extremely ticklish, and this sort of treatment would have had me on the ceiling screaming. But Sadie somehow had relaxed me, and was methodically washing first one foot, and then the other, her freakishly long and agile tongue darting between my toes, her teeth nibbling at my calluses as she reached them.

Steve, upon discovering this little scene, thought it all very amusing, especially since I had made such a terrible fuss about him feeding Sadie off his dinner plate. He couldn't help but make great fun of me.

"Well, at least now you don't have to take a shower," he said. "Sadie's getting you nice and clean, I see."

"Go away," I said, raising my head. "I like this."

And I did. There was something so utterly comforting and relaxing about being sniffed, and licked, and tended by a tiny lapdog. It was like having a massage, or getting your hair done.

Sometimes Sadie slept with Steve and me, instead of with Daniel. (We actually joked that she "slept around" at night. She went to bed with whoever happened to be taking care of her.) When she was in our bed, Sadie would sleep wedged between Steve and me for warmth, or curled up against one of our pillows near our heads. I would wake in the middle of the night, or in the morning, to find her sniffing my ear or cheek, or licking my armpit. Steve did, too. Somewhere along the way, we had let our guards down and allowed this newest member of our family to impose her own habits upon us.

I especially noticed this at night, when a strange wildness often seemed to settle over our bed whenever Sadie was there. I have never slept all the way through the night, and I usually have an hour or two of staring at the ceiling sometime between two and four in the morning. And now I would wake, moonlight spilling through the bedroom window, and find Sadie beside me, twitching and growling and barking in her sleep.

She seemed to regress to a more primal, wolfish state as she slept, and she appeared in her dreams to be out hunting with other wild dogs or with her wolfish forebears, bringing down deer or other game, or chasing off marauding bands of intruders. On some level, it was perhaps silly or even delusional, for a tiny lapdog like Sadie to dream of hunting or of biting strangers, her tiny near-toothless gums banging together. It was around this time, though, that I happened to read more about these tiny lapdogs and where they came from—and I began to take her wolfish ways more seriously.

Dig into the literature of any small or toy-breed of dog and you will find yourself immersed (as I did) in stories of how ancient that breed is, and how that particular kind of dog guarded ancient temples or sat on the laps of kings. It is claimed, for example, that Maltese dogs like Sadie date back at least to Greek and Roman times, and that the Roman governor Publius of Malta (or Melitiae) had a Maltese dog named Issa around 40 AD. This little lapdog was so beloved that Publius's friend, the poet Martial, wrote poems to her. These verses, roughly translated, go: *Issa is more frolicsome than Cotulia's canary/Issa is more pure than a white dove's kiss*, and so forth. You get the idea.

These days I teach creative writing, and I know how exaggerated family stories tend to be passed down, and to improve with each retelling. In fact, I have always tended to dismiss these purebred dog "legends" as a lot of hooey. I'm not saying that a poet didn't write verses to a little white dog back in Roman times. That's pretty well documented. I'm just saying that I was rather skeptical that this little white dog, whoever she was, had any real connection to the toy breed we know today as "the Maltese."

What I learned, however, looking into it, is that modern genetics has given fresh credence to the notion that our tiny lapdogs are actually quite ancient, and are descended rather directly from grey wolves.

The domestication of dogs is generally placed in the Middle East around 12,000-16,000 years ago.[2] DNA testing shows that all dogs are descended from the same set of Middle Eastern grey wolves and share much of their genetic material. Some biologists have argued that dogs probably "self-domesticated" as camp scavengers, with the more tame and less fearful wolves being better tolerated around human encampments, and therefore being more successful in their relations with humans. In any event, it is pretty well agreed these days that an animal we would recognize as "the modern dog" came into being by 12,000 years ago, and that such canines served as hunting dogs, guarding dogs, and herders.

---

[2] I should note here that the exact mechanism by which dogs came to be domesticated from wolves, and the precise dates for that domestication, are currently matters of heated debate among biologists, many of whom come armed with fresh-breaking DNA research. Some biologists and science writers have argued for a much earlier date of domestication in Europe, based upon discoveries of proto-dog remains found in pre-historic caves. However, the weight of current opinion holds that domestication of the dog in Europe was interrupted by the ice age that set in 19,000 to 27,000 years ago, and so the ultimate domestication of the dog probably took place in Mesolithic villages in the Middle East between 12,000 and 16,000 years ago. The thing that becomes clear, looking at the current research, is that the story of the domestication of the dog is a complicated one, with many false fits and starts, and that modern genetics will likely shed further light on that process in the coming years.

"The Call Of The Small"

What is interesting for our purposes is that small dogs appear to have arisen not long after this. There are remains of small dogs from the Middle East dating to 10,000-12,000 years ago that resemble small terriers, so the first small dogs appear very ancient indeed. And genetics research reveals that small dogs, from Pom to Peke, share a specific gene that retards growth called insulin-like growth factor 1. Nearly all small dogs, it turns out, have this specific piece of DNA inhibiting their growth. Because little dogs share this common gene, the mutation presumably occurred quite early on in the development of smaller dogs, and contemporary tiny and toy dog breeds are all pretty much believed to have descended from this one ancient gene pool of Middle Eastern small terriers.

Less discussed is the fact that this early point of origin for small dogs coincides with a time when Middle Eastern societies were moving from a hunter-gatherer way of life to more sedentary and agriculturally-based communities. Small dogs may have been used, like cats, as "ratters" to keep rodents away from grain stores. However, the small dog's early origins would have placed it alongside the domestication of other wild animals such as cattle, pigs and goats, all of which had a reduced body size upon domestication and were used as food sources. It therefore seems likely that small dogs were bred, at least at first, as much for their meat and fur as for their companionship or rodent dispatching skills.

In fact, it is probably not a coincidence that the very oldest Middle Eastern and Asian dog breeds, such as the Pug, Shih Tzu, Lhasa Apso and Peke, all have the short stubby legs and thick fatty bodies that you would expect to find in a meat-producing animal. Ancient Chinese writings from the Zhou Dynasty refer to "three beasts" bred for food, including the pig, goat, and dog. In European societies, horses and dogs eventually fell under the "cannibalism taboo," a social custom prohibiting them from being consumed as food, which may have arisen as early as the 8th Century. However, this "taboo" has always slipped during times of scarcity, even in the West. And the cannibalism taboo has never been adopted in many parts of the world where horses and dogs are still widely used for human and pet food.

Artwork from intervening eras provides pictorial proof for the continuity of small dog breeds since ancient times. Chinese art, for example, shows that the Pekingese or "Lion Dog," bred to resemble Chinese Temple Guardian Lions, have barely changed in nearly 2,000 years. And 8th Century Chinese art abounds with images of Pekes and Shih Tzus, which were prized as house pets during the Ming Dynasty. There is a tiny dog that looks a lot like a Chihuahua in Botticelli's "The Trials of Moses," a fresco in the Sistine Chapel dating from 1480-82, shortly before Columbus made his voyages to the new world.

As for Maltese dogs, they first appear on Greek Amphora as far back as 500 BC, and Aristotle mentions "Melitaie Catelli," the Maltese dog's Latin name, around 370 BC. Strabo, in the First Century, identifies a small white breed of dog from Malta as being "favored by the noblewomen," at around the same time as Martial wrote his verses to Issa. The breed crops up again later in Europe, as the "Ancient Dogs of Malta." Maltese dogs apparently were imported to Britain during the reign of King Henry the VIII, and during

Elizabethan times were dubbed "the comforter," and were worn along with other small lapdogs as "sleeve dogs" in the voluminous balloon sleeves of ladies dresses fashionable during the late Renaissance.

The impression of small dogs like Sadie that emerges from all of this historical and biological evidence is that of a Middle Eastern grey wolf, downsized by a genetic fluke, and then used as a food source until it was able to worm its way into the homes and hearts of humans—eventually convincing those same humans to ban everyone from eating them. You can see why some researchers have called dogs the most successful "social parasites" the world has ever seen.

Once you begin to understand small lapdogs as the rather direct descendants of Middle Eastern grey wolves, you also begin to appreciate their wild, instinctive ways a whole lot more, or so I found. You start to realize that all of that licking and tending probably has to do with pack solidarity rituals that you—knowingly or otherwise—are participating in rather intimately with your little dog. You also begin to see that these small dogs' dreams of hunting are quite real and vivid to them. In their dreams, these tiny animals are probably out under the stars at night, on a stretch of desert, bringing down deer and other game with their wolfish brethren.

Sometimes late at night, I would gaze down at Sadie sleeping beside me, twitching and growling and chewing, and I would imagine the blanched sheets of our bed as a stretch of desert sand upon which we roamed, hunting in moonlight. At those moments Sadie would sometimes emit a long low howl in her sleep that seemed filled with all of the wild loneliness and desolation of a true wolf. I would feel the hair rise on the back of my own neck, and hear my heart thump a little faster in my ears—and I would think it both funny and rather thrilling—to be lying there in a pool of moonlight, keeping company with my tiny white wolf.

Chapter 13

THE END OF THE HONEYMOON

If I had hoped that Tessa Piero would visit Sadie once, and that would be the end of it, I was only fooling myself. The pretty girl with the cold eyes visited regularly for the rest of the summer, usually once a week when she had play dates with the other girls on the point. On those occasions when she missed her weekly visit—if she had some other commitment or whatever—my hopes would soar that perhaps our entanglement with the Piero kids was over, finished, done. But then, a week later, sure as rain in New England, there would be the three girls knocking at our door again, and Sadie would be howling to go out with them like a shrimp-sized banshee.

I tried to be gracious to Tessa each time she appeared "to take Sadie out," but the young girl wanted nothing to do with me. She let her two pals do the talking, and did her own best to ignore me, determined apparently not to acknowledge me as Sadie's new owner. For the most part she said not a word to me, and tried at all cost to avoid meeting my eyes. The three girls always took Sadie away with them—A few polite comments from the other two, and they would be out the door, and off to the Marstens' house or to the other friend's house on the point.

After a few such visits, I began to feel very frustrated with the whole situation—Not least because, each time Tessa presented herself at my door, and took Sadie out for the afternoon, it felt to me as if she was trying to drag me down into some ragged place in the soul—into that existential place where parents die—where everyone you have ever loved will someday be dead. A waking nightmare of a place.

It wasn't her fault, of course—This ten year old girl couldn't know what had happened in my life, or how such things can come back to haunt you, and make you behave in strange and unaccountable ways. Having endured the horror of losing my own father when I was not much older than she was now, and more recently having lost my mother, I was not up to this situation. And yet, I was stuck with it, enmeshed in it, mired in it—And each time I heard the high musical voices of the three girls outside my front door, it seemed as if they were pulling me back somewhere I didn't want to go, yet somewhere I couldn't help going.

It all made me inappropriately angry; made me want to lash out at this young girl with her chilly eyes. I would think, *What's wrong with this kid? Doesn't she get it? Sadie is no longer her dog.*

I would also, after Tessa left, get mad at Bob Piero. Enough was enough. Where was the parental presence here? Why wasn't Piero intervening, and cutting this visiting thing off. The kid wasn't getting her dog back. What good was stringing her along? Or so I thought of it at the time. And then the anxiety would rise in my throat again—that I was being used by the Pieros as a glorified dog sitter until they could get settled in their new home.

And worse, I couldn't even discuss the matter with Steve and Dan because they were still so angry with me for even letting Tessa come and see Sadie. In fact, I was now actually taking affirmative steps to hide the girl's visits from them.

Oh, what a mess.

Steve, of course, easily sussed out that Tessa was still visiting. I have never been able to lie to my husband about anything. He can always tell when I'm omitting or withholding information about my day. He's a lawyer. He doesn't hesitate to cross-examine me. He can tell when I'm leaving things out. Or avoiding things. He probes. Tessa's visits always came out.

"Look, just tell her she can't have the dog back," he half-shouted at me one day.

"I know," I said. "I know."

"That's really quite enough," he said.

"You're right," I agreed.

It was.

But I couldn't. I couldn't say that to Tessa.

For reasons that I didn't fully understand, I was incapable of disengaging myself from this young girl, or of facing the situation in an appropriate and adult way.

How could I explain to my husband what was going on inside of me? That this was about me processing something that had happened long ago. That it was about losing a parent and then a dog; was about the strange fascination of watching the Piero kids going through the same things I once had.

They say that there is no such thing as an unmixed motivation. Mine were thoroughly confused.

I think that I was bound up in the terrible allure of watching the Piero kids going down the same vortex I once had. But I also wanted to help them as well. I wanted somehow to keep them from the same pain I had suffered. Too, I wanted to be done with them. On some level, I never wanted to have to see them, ever again. Yet I couldn't look away. I couldn't just cut the whole thing off, as I probably should have done.

All of this is simply to say that I had very little insight into my own behavior at that point. I should have found a clue that there was something very much amiss with my reactions in the flares of anger I felt towards Tessa, and my increasing vexation with her father. I kept wanting Bob Piero to step in and do something, which of course never happened.

Later I would wonder if Bob Piero even knew about Tessa's visits to Sadie, or if those visits were just something the bus stop mothers on the point were organizing to keep up an air of normalcy for the kids that summer following Calista's death. At the time, though, I was fixated on Bob Piero. I wanted for a parent to step in and do the right thing, something that I had perhaps waited for in my own youth, after my father's death—a futile desire. Bob Piero would never step in, and looking back on it today, I'm not even sure he was aware of what was going on with his daughter and Sadie. The little dog was out of sight and out of mind. He had other things on his hands.

The situation was in my hands. And I—I seemed unable to respond.

As the summer wore on, another challenge began to surface as well. Sadie's behavior began to degenerate in unexpected ways. It was bad enough, having her screeching and rushing the door when anyone came by, as she had done with Alice. But now she began attacking other, larger dogs when we were out walking, as she had formerly done with Willow. One of my dog-walking friends, Erin, was shocked to have her own two big dogs attacked by this tiny Maltese, and began referring to Sadie as "the little pitbull," which I could see was probably a bad sign.

At first I tried just to laugh it off. Sadie had so few remaining teeth that the sight of her attempting to sink her gums into the leg of a big Golden retriever or a Lab was not only shocking, it was also rather funny. Usually the larger dog would merely look down at her with a mild expression of annoyance, and brush her off as if she were a mosquito or a fly. However, since Sadie was also snarling and growling and trying to bite with every inch of her tiny body, it seemed as if eventually she would meet some large mean dog that was not amused, and that this dog would pick her up and shake her until she lay limp in his jaws. And so I began to fear that Sadie was putting herself in real danger.

The other thing that was happening was that Sadie was now beginning to challenge the other members of my household. These kinds of dominance issues can be a real problem with smaller dogs, because—as I have noted—we humans tend not to react to them as we would with a larger dog. If a German Shepherd was standing on your lap and growling at you, you would certainly do something about it. But if a tiny Chihuahua does the same thing, you tend not to take it terribly seriously.

These lapdogs are so small, that you simply do reflexively as I had done with Sadie. You scoop them up, jam them under an arm, and put a hand over the dog's muzzle. There's not much a five-pounder can do when squeezed under an arm, feet off the ground, and gagged in this way. The trouble is that the longer this behavior is ignored, the longer it goes unchecked, the more of a problem it can become.

Sadie never actually tried to challenge me—She never tried to take on "her new momma"—(She wouldn't have dared, I thought). However, she was now growling at Steve and Dan, especially when food was around, or if there was a favored place on the couch or bed she wanted to "guard" as hers.

What was going on here? I wondered. Sadie had always had issues with other dogs, but she had been so good with people up until now—had always been very sweet-tempered and affectionate.

Unbeknownst to me, though, we were running into what animal rescue people call "the end of the honeymoon." Rescued dogs usually are on their best behavior when they are first adopted, and they are settling into their new home. This is known as the "honeymoon period," when the dog is currying favor with its new family, and desperately wants approval and acceptance. However, after a few weeks or months, everyone starts to relax and to become accustomed to the new family configuration. It is at this point that a rescued dog's "true personality" often starts to emerge, and he or she often begins "testing" his or her position in "the new pack."

Sadie apparently was now feeling sufficiently comfortable with us to let her true stripes show, and she was proving to be something of a little bully.

I told Steve and Dan "not to let Sadie growl at them" and to flip her on her back if she snarled or snapped, just the way Willow did with her. However, these guys were both pretty mild mannered themselves, and they rarely followed through on disciplining Sadie unless I was right there with them, and instructing them on what to do.

In retrospect, I can't really blame them. Nobody wants to handle a growling, snapping dog, even a very tiny one.

Then, one night we were all crowded in Steve's and my bed, reading bedtime stories. Sadie was reclining beside me, part of this cozy family grouping. We finished up reading, and Dan leaned over to give me a goodnight kiss before heading off to his own bedroom. As he leaned over me—suddenly and without warning—Sadie went for his upper arm, and bit my son, pinching the flesh between his armpit and elbow in her two remaining fangs.

"Owwww!" Dan cried loudly, and sprang back holding his arm.

Everyone was suddenly standing up and shouting, "NO!"

And then we all stood about in shocked silence, while Sadie sheepishly tried to sink into the bedcovers—though I must say she did not look half as contrite as she probably ought to have.

Steve and I examined Dan's arm. Sadie had not broken the skin, but she had left a good scrape and two deep pink pin-like marks upon Daniel's arm. (Poor Dan was gazing at Sadie with betrayal in his eyes.)

That was it, I thought. I finally saw how I had been ignoring Sadie's bad behavior because she was so small. We all had. It hadn't seemed as if she was likely to do any real harm with the few remaining teeth she had left. But this was the last straw. I was not going to have my son bitten.

Some serious dog training was clearly in order. I didn't care how tiny the dog might be.

In retrospect, I can see that it took us far too long to get Sadie into dog training. I had underestimated her because she was so tiny. How hard could it be to handle an animal that weighed only five pounds, I had thought. However, that was really no excuse. I had done lots of dog training before in my life, with Willow and with the other dogs I'd had, and I should have known better, and nipped Sadie's bad habits in the bud.

Also, knowing what I do now about rescued dogs, I would put any dog I got in a rescue situation into training much sooner—as soon as the dog had recovered enough to participate. When we got Sadie, I didn't know about the "honeymoon period" or about the process whereby a rescued animal settles into its new home. I understand now, though, that appropriate and positive training can actually assist a rescued dog in forming good relations within its new family unit, and in finding its place within the new pecking order. It was work that we had avoided doing with Sadie until now, and we were badly overdue.

Chapter 14

TRAINING THE SMALL DOG

Over the past ten or so years, the training of small lapdogs seems—for reasons having to do with the growth of celebrity media culture—to have fallen largely to the ranks of what I shall call, for lack of a better term, "celebrity dog trainers." By this I mean either dog trainers who have attached themselves to big-name celebrities like Oprah or Madonna, or trainers who have themselves become celebrities in their own right by dint of being featured on "reality" television shows. A number of these series have come and gone where a dog trainer goes around solving the true life problems of "real people" and their misbehaving smaller dogs—troubles not unlike those that Steve, Dan and I had been having with Sadie.

    I place the term "real people" in quotations because many of the folks featured on these shows often seem anything but. I suppose it would be a bit hypocritical for a memoirist like me to complain about people airing the intimate details of their lives on national television in a scripted or premeditated way. Still, I think what bothers me about these shows is the near super-human ability of these supposedly "real people" to stand for hours in unquestioning and open-mouthed awe at the advice being dispensed by their celebrated dog-gurus, no matter how far-fetched that advice might appear to be.

The celebrity dog-training trend is, I suppose, not surprising. There has been, as I have noted, a strong connection between celebrities and small lapdogs since at least the early aughts—from these dogs' initial popularity on the arms of entertainers like Paris Hilton and Jessica Simpson—to the colorful antics of celebrity dog trainers like Cesar Millan, whose thick dark hair and preternaturally white teeth and inch-deep dimples seem to have mesmerized his largely small dog owning audience into overlooking the fact that his background was in dog-grooming and limo driving, and not in animal behavior.

Dog training is actually quite a scientific discipline these days, though you would never know it from watching reality TV. The celebrity dog trainers on these programs almost invariably dish out advice clothed in an alluring veil of smoke and mystery, using terms like "dog whispering" and suggesting the intervention of magic, or perhaps the paranormal. The real trouble with many of these trainers is that, if you observe them closely, you begin to detect that their purportedly magical curatives often involve things like pinching the dog, to hissing at it, and using choke and prong collars, forced marches, and sometimes even shock collars.

Leaving aside for the moment the questionable rationale of selecting a dog trainer based upon the whiteness of his teeth, the depth of his dimples, or his tenuous connection to Oprah, the real issue with such training advice is that it is often punitive in nature, and is based upon dog training methods that have been largely discredited in recent years by animal behaviorists. The fact is, this is exactly what dog training *used to be like* back in the bad old days of the "military style" dog training that came out of the two world wars, and was later promoted by trainers like Bill Koehler, and others. However by the 1980s and 1990s, a new generation of more scientific and humane dog trainers came on the scene, and showed everyone that harsh or punitive dog training methods not only were extremely unkind to the animals, but also were terribly ineffective.

I was fortunate to be aware of the progress in dog training area at the time we were looking to train Sadie back in 2002, and so I knew better than to be sucked into this growing celebrity dog training craze that was just getting started back then. Before Willow had developed his arthritis, I had done a year of agility training with him that is chronicled in my book *Teaching the Dog to Think*. I had been brought up with the old, harsh military style of dog training myself, and was well-acquainted with those methods, and I had found it an eye opening (if rather humiliating) experience to work with some of the new behaviorally-based trainers—who regarded my old harsh training tactics as rather bone-headed, if not sadistic.

In *Teaching the Dog to Think*, I trace the history of dog training in this country, and detail my experiences coming around to the kinder and far more effective dog training methods, often dubbed "positive training" or "clicker training." I shall therefore not repeat that information here. However, I strongly encourage you to read my earlier memoir if at any point you are inclined to pinch, hiss at, strike, choke, or shock your little lapdog based upon something that you have seen on TV.

Such treatment of smaller dogs is, first and foremost, dangerous—These dogs are so tiny that they are easily injured. Also the genetic dwarfism that produces their small frames makes them much more prone to spinal and joint injuries than are larger dogs. Harsh treatment in dog training is also, as I had learned in training with Willow, completely unnecessary.

For our purposes here, let me simply sum up what I had taken away from our earlier training. Behaviorally-based animal trainers, like Karen Pryor the famous dolphin trainer, and others, have shown beyond all doubt that the most effective way to train a dog is by slowly building skills and wanted behaviors through the reinforcement and "shaping" of those behaviors using food rewards. The old "punitive" methods are good only for "shutting the dog down," and even then those methods quickly wear out. They are next to useless at teaching skills and building good habits over the long haul.

It actually isn't all that hard to see why punitive training methods, like shouting "no" or hissing, aren't going to work on a smart, hard-headed little dog like Sadie, at least not for very long. A loud "no" might set her back the first time, but she would quickly become inured to being shouted at, and her trainer (me, in this case) would only have to "escalate" by shouting "no" louder and louder. You often see this escalation phenomenon with punitive training tactics. The dog nearly always becomes accustomed to being shouted at, or to having its neck jerked with a choke collar. Just ask anyone you see being dragged around your local conservation area by a large dog on a choke collar and leash. *How's that choke collar working for you, buddy?* Trust me, the dog just gets used to it.

Unless, that is, you are willing to actually harm your dog (*and shame on you if you are!*) Otherwise, you are only going to prove yourself more and more ineffectual to your dog by using harsh dog training methods. And do you really want to be using punitive training tactics on a tiny lapdog? Or on a rescued dog that has already been traumatized?

The same is true of "pack dominance" methods such as flipping a dog like Sadie on her back—which you will notice I made the mistake of recommending to Steve and Dan. (Old habits die hard.) That might scare Sadie once or twice, and reinforce my superior role in the short term—but it was unlikely to work for any lengthier period of time if I didn't actually hurt her. (In fact, that's why this strategy worked somewhat better for Willow, than for me, since he made it clear, by snapping at Sadie, that he was willing to bite her—though you will notice that even he mostly tried just to avoid her, by going outside to his tie-out under the pine tree.)

No, unless you are willing to inflict actual pain or injury on your tiny lapdog, such "pack dominance" methods are of limited and diminishing value. Over time you only prove to your small dog that you aren't really the one in charge. And why would you use such methods anyway, when you can swiftly get your small dog working happily with you, and executing your every command, simply by using a handful of tasty treats?

―――

Having said all of this, I must confess that I found it much harder to train a small lapdog than it had been to train a big dog like Willow. Sadie was very tiny and lively, and she was always extremely difficult to control. I was used to training bigger, slower-moving, and much more obliging dogs like Willow. Sadie, though, was a different story. She was a determined little dog, with a good bit of the terrier in her, and she always wanted to do things her own way. She also moved so fast, that it was often hard to keep up with her.

If I asked Sadie to "sit"—someone had clearly acquainted her with this word previously—she would sit, lay down, roll-over, and sit again, all within the space of about a second and a half. Should I reward such behavior? I wondered. She had sat. Twice, in fact. But it wasn't as if I was establishing much control over her.

And, in truth, Sadie wasn't trying very hard, at least not at first. It looked to me at the time as if she was just "throwing behaviors" at me in the hopes that a treat would fall her way.

She was even worse with Daniel. If he told her to sit she would gaze at him rather deliberately, and then come and sit pointedly in front of me. It was exactly as if she were saying to him, *Look, son, I'll work for momma, but not for you.*

The other problem we were having, training Sadie, was that most of the treats we tried—hamburgers or jerky treats—seemed to fill her up too quickly. Tiny dogs have equally tiny stomachs, and no matter how small we broke up her treats, it seemed as if Sadie was soon "full"—and was no longer interested in working with us.

Looking back on it, I think that Sadie wasn't as excited as another dog might have been about human food, since Steve was feeding her rotisserie chicken off his dinner plate nearly every night.

Clearly Dan and I needed some training help, and training help specifically geared to smaller dogs. Especially Dan—He was still furious with Sadie for biting him, though he was not complaining too loudly about it, because I think he still feared I would get rid of her. I, though, was somewhat confident that training could help, since I had had good results before, with Willow.

I asked around among my dog walking friends and my agility pals, and soon I located a positive agility trainer west of Boston who was starting a dog training class specifically for smaller dogs. I then dragged Sadie and Dan off to dog training class with me, both—I should add—somewhat against their wills.

Our new trainer was a wheelchair agility competitor whom we shall call Bill Sellers. Bill was a wry, patient fellow—not as hard-driven as some of the other agility trainers that Willow and I had worked with—but fully as effective. And Bill had his own interest in starting this small dog training class—because he had a new and very lively Papillion puppy, and he was starting to see for himself the special issues involved in training a tiny lapdog.

Bill took one look at Sadie and me, doing our training routine, and started to laugh and wheel his chair towards us for more instruction. "She's trying to train you," he called.

This, I quickly realized, was quite true. No matter what I asked her to do, Sadie always tried putting her own spin on things. Her own little variation that said, "I'm in charge here, not you."

Bill explained that I was going to have to be very careful about what I rewarded Sadie for, so that I didn't end up simply rewarding her for "having her own way."

It was actually another student in our class who solved our "treat problem" for us. I was complaining loudly one day about how hard Sadie was to control, and how quickly her tummy "filled up." A woman in the class took me aside and suggested that I try "string cheese." This person had a fleet of three tiny "teacup Poms." (They looked like tiny toy teddy bears, and ran their agility courses in unison, which was very cute.) These dogs were even smaller than Sadie, and had to have tinier stomachs than she did

"Why string cheese?" I asked.

"Just try it," the woman said, with a curt and knowledgeable nod of her chin.

To be honest, I didn't really even know back then what string cheese was. I guess I knew that it was a popular snack item, but I usually tried to avoid processed cheese products—and this stuff had always looked to me like processed cheese. It was tube-shaped, having clearly been produced by an extruder in some sort of industrial process, and it came wrapped in plastic like that other suspicious cheese product, American cheese.

What I did not know at the time was that string cheese is actually a legitimate cheese. It is just a very dense, high-fat, low-moisture mozzarella that is pulled into long strings at the curding stage of cheese-making, giving it its characteristic dry and stringy quality that makes it easy to handle, less messy, and more practical for things like school lunches and—apparently, as I was learning—dog training.

In any event, we were desperate to try anything that might work on Sadie. And so I decided to give string cheese a try. I went out and bought several varieties that I found at our local grocery store, and brought them to training class. I hoped it would work. Dan was starting to complain that dog training was "boring" and that Sadie was "too dumb to learn anything." Sadie also, given her inattention to us, was starting to focus on the other dogs in the class, and was beginning to growl at them—an ominous sign.

You will have to believe me when I say that string cheese was some sort of miracle. It was as if Sadie had discovered her own personal nirvana, her drug, her lust. She was like a meth addict for string cheese. There was nothing she wouldn't do to get at it. Forgotten were the other dogs; gone was her lazy tossing off of behaviors. We now had her full attention. She was sitting in front of me as if the act of sitting was a salute.

And when Dan held the string cheese, she dashed straight for him, and saluted him, too.

Dan actually turned out to be a much better dog trainer for Sadie than I was. I was hampered by my past of training bigger dogs, and continued to look for slower and more controlled behaviors to reward. Dan, though, had no such preconceived notions of how dog training ought to go. He sped right past all of the "control-oriented" obedience commands I was used to, like sit, down and stay, and went right for the exuberant circus dog tricks, such as getting Sadie to dance on her hind legs, or hop like a bunny, or twirl in a little circus dog spin. They also practiced high-fiving, and getting Sadie to play dead, after being "shot" by Dan with his finger-gun.

If I had known then what I know now, I would have started Sadie in training much sooner, shortly after we got her, and well before her "honeymoon period" was over. Training her was a wonderful reminder to me of why positive reinforcement and operant conditioning work so well. In the world of dogs, it is he who controls the best treats who wins.

When Dan was just another member of our household, Sadie gave him no respect at all. But the moment she had to perform for my son to get the good treats out of his hands, suddenly there was nothing she wouldn't do for him. Dan was now all-powerful in her eyes, the king of the roost—He had the string cheese!!

And Dan was enjoying his newfound power over this little imp. I remember him giving me a big grin as he put Sadie through her paces at home again and again. I could only stand back and laugh as I watched the two of them careen around the living room, practicing their dog training—Sadie spiraling about on her hind legs, dancing for Dan and howling for string cheese, as she threw him high fives with her front paws.

Chapter 15

DANIEL

My recollection of the Fall of 2002 is rather hazy, but one thing stands out in my memory—I rather belatedly realized that Tessa Piero had stopped visiting. We were actually a few weeks into the new school year before I suddenly took note of the fact that we that hadn't seen the girl in a couple of weeks. I don't know why this fact didn't register right away with me, since this was what I had been waiting for—for Tessa to give up on her little dog.

Steve's intransigence about giving Sadie back was beginning to wear on me. I sort of understood his position. He was still furious with the Pieros that they had nearly killed his little friend, and his sense of moral outrage had not diminished over time as Sadie became more and more "our dog." Unlike me, however, Steve was not prepared to parse the moral responsibility for this perceived outrage between the "two innocent children" and the "adults involved." It was all very simple in his view. The Pieros had shown they couldn't properly care for Sadie, end of story.

Daniel's growing attachment to Sadie also made it seem more critical that we keep her. The two of them, boy and dog, had bonded in dog training, and the biting incident was now a thing of the past. They were now closer than they had ever been. Sadie was very much Dan's dog—at least until Steve got home at night and took out the rotisserie chicken. And Dan had—on a few occasions—witnessed Sadie going off with Tessa and her friends and barking shrilly with excitement—and he had been absolutely furious. "It's so unfair!" Oh, how that phrase still echoes in my ears.

Dan was now parroting everything his father said about the Pieros not getting Sadie back. "They had their chance to kill her. Let them get another dog to kill," and so forth.

All of this is to say that I should have been overjoyed when Tessa ceased in her weekly visits. My failing to notice was, I think, simply a result of the fact that we were so crazily busy that fall, so that Tessa's absence did not immediately sink in.

That was a big year for our little family. Daniel had just finished out his last year at his old Montessori school, which ended at third grade. We had enrolled him for the fall at a new Montessori school that went through middle school. This new school had some great experienced teachers, and we were excited about having Dan start there. However, when Dan showed up to begin fourth grade in September, the experienced teachers we had previously liked so well had all vanished—There had been some sort of shakeup in the upper-level classrooms. And in their place were several teachers who were very new to teaching, and only one remaining teacher was still Montessori certified.

We let Dan start at the school anyway. We had paid a large deposit to this tony private school running into the thousands of dollars, and it seemed as if we ought at least

Daniel

to give it a shot. As soon as school began, however, my bright, sensitive son found himself in a large unruly classroom, full of fourth through sixth graders in the charge of brand new teachers, and he hated it. All was confusion and tears each day after school—over homework assignments, uncertain curricula, and 6th grade boys hazing the younger students without any apparent hindrance from the adults on the scene. After two weeks of this, it was clear that things were not working out.

In desperation, Steve and I put in an offer on a condo in Hingham, where we had already been looking for a new home anyway, and a few weeks into the term we started Dan in public school there. After the confusion of the Montessori school, the structure of public school came as a great relief. There was a curriculum! There were clear homework assignments! And a cheerful, accessible principal to handle discipline problems! And, best of all, Dan's new fourth-grade teacher—appropriately named "Mrs. Fine,"—was one of those brilliant, experienced teachers who somehow can tame a wild classroom that is full of antsy fourth-grade boys, and make everything work beautifully.

We were terribly relieved to have Dan land in such a good situation, but it was not the end of our troubles that fall. We had been allowed to start our son in public school in Hingham because we had a signed purchase and sale agreement on a condo in the town. However, the closing ended up being delayed because the seller had unexpectedly filed for bankruptcy, and court approvals were required in order to close on the sale. Meanwhile, we were still living in Marshfield, and I was still driving Dan to and from school in Hingham each day.

With all that was going on in our lives, Tessa Piero and her visits were no longer foremost in my mind. She had been returning Sadie, after all, and it no longer seemed as if she would just run off with the dog on us. It was only after I realized, somewhat belatedly in early October, that the girl's visits had stopped that the Piero kids again seemed to become an issue—at least in my own mind.

Why wasn't it a relief that Tessa was no longer visiting? Wasn't that what I'd been waiting for? It's a little hard for me to explain today why this realization somehow had precisely the opposite affect upon me.

To me, Tessa's absence meant that she had probably—like my son Daniel—started school in her new district, and so she had less time to visit her friends on the point, and less of an opportunity to see Sadie. This also meant, though, that the Pieros were probably either out of their summer rental and into their new home in Norwell, or that they were about to move there.

It seemed to me, in short, that if the Pieros were ever going to want Sadie back, it was likely to be now.

But I didn't hear a peep from them. And the silence was deafening. I kept waiting in the afternoon for the sound of Tessa's anxious feet on our front doorstep, as I had heard them so many times before. I kept listening for that soft, little-girl knocking on the front door. And for the voices of her friends.

In this context, it was doubly maddening that we couldn't just close on the condo, and move away to Hingham. *Leave the scene already!* It seemed to me as if we couldn't close on the condo fast enough. And yet the closing dragged out, as my lawyer husband slowly negotiated the necessary bankruptcy formalities and tried to move the transaction towards completion.

Daniel

I remember at one point discussing my frustration with my friend Erin, who suggested we "hide" Sadie at her house—just until our family could make the move to Hingham. I remember feeling very torn by this suggestion. That was one approach, I supposed. But it felt very underhanded. It felt, in fact, like dog-stealing.

It also felt rather infantile and preposterous. Hiding a little lapdog from a ten-year-old? Seriously?

As usual, I ended up doing nothing. As before, I still felt bound up by my promise to give the Pieros their dog back in six months. I was still as "stuck" as ever, and still at odds with my own family.

What I did not realize was that there was someone else in our household upon whom this whole situation was wearing as much as it was wearing on me. I didn't realize at the time how much stress all of this "not knowing about Sadie" was causing Daniel. But Sadie was now his best friend, especially given his change of school systems, which had left my son a bit adrift socially. And after all this time he was sick and tired of hearing me talk about the promises I had made to give Sadie back.

With the new competence of a public school fourth-grader, and unbeknownst to me, Daniel started keeping track of the "six months" that the Piero kids had to reclaim their dog. He was counting the days and months on the big "family calendar" we kept in a permanent place of prominence on our large dining room table.

Apparently this was information that he planned to use to confront me at some point. Of course, I would only find out about this later.

Chapter 16

"SMALL DOGS NEED CLOTHES"

The other thing that I recall from the Fall of 2002, besides Tessa disappearing, is that I finally came to grips with my late mother's disapproval of small dogs. The occasion for this was that our groomer, Kate, had insisted on "mowing off" the remainder of Sadie's "bad old coat" from the time when she had been malnourished. This made sense to do because Sadie's new coat was growing in much thicker and whiter. What was left of her old coat now stood out from her body in drab wisps, as if she were a Dr. Seuss creature in need of a good combing. So, despite some qualms, I agree to the short haircut Kate wanted to give Sadie. But when I picked up my little dog up from Kate's grooming salon, I was shocked to see that she was nearly shaved.

Okay, it wasn't quite that bad. I'm exaggerating a little—Sadie still had some fur left, a short white frizzy clip. And Kate assured me that our little dog would "coat up" for winter, which she in fact did.

Still, the haircut was a shock for the poor little thing. The weather in New England was still warm and glorious during the day, in September and early October, but it was starting to grow cooler in the evenings. And Sadie was beginning to shiver again—just the way I remembered her shivering when we first got her back in June, when she had almost no fur at all. I was starting to have to tuck her in my jacket again, and to turn up the heat in the house to keep her warm enough.

I remember going to a dinner party one evening around this time, with some writer friends, and complaining that this little dog of mine was always cold, was always shivering. How pathetic she was, I said. One of my friends at the party had recently gotten a Chihuahua herself, and was aghast to hear this statement coming out of my mouth. Chihuahuas have very little fur, and so this friend was already well into the dog couture. She asked me, in a rather shocked tone, "Don't you have any clothes for Sadie?" As in, *What's wrong with you, gal? Are you crazy?* "Small dogs need clothes!" she cried. "You must immediately get her something to wear!"

I felt rather stupid when my friend said this. Of course Sadie needed clothes. It was yet another moment that I felt quite clueless about little lapdogs.

It had been early summer when we'd gotten Sadie, and as the summer had progressed it was, if anything, too hot outside. So I hadn't had to deal with this whole issue of dog clothing. And I think that on some level I was avoiding buying Sadie anything to wear because of my late mother's presumed disapproval. Dog clothing seemed like the last bastion of the "frivolous" small dog lifestyle that my mother had so long ago taken note of.

I had actually already come somewhat to terms with my mother's disapproval in wrestling with my own self-image after Alice's visit. However, I was pretty sure that putting clothes on a tiny lapdog like Sadie would have sent my mother—if not the entire rest of our upstate New York clan—right over the top. Plainly I was striving to turn myself into, if not a Mrs. LeBlanc now, then some sort of Paris Hilton type of person.

However, with the New England temperatures plummeting and Sadie shivering and cringing in the cold, I was going to have to suck it up. I was going to have to go out and buy some tiny little dog clothes.

If you have ever been clothes shopping with a small dog, then you will know that it is not as easy as it sounds.

After all, how hard could it be? You find a little sweater. Boom, you're done. Not hard, right?

Wrong.

The problem with these clothes is that they are made for dogs, not for people. So the clothes tend not to be very well made. They tend to be made of scratchy, inflexible materials—inferior materials, really—which is why they have ended up in dog clothing in the first place.

This turns out to be a real problem, because what you really need in a dog coat is a flexible, stretchy, breathable material—because the dog will be wearing the coat outdoors and will be exercising in it. What you are really looking for in a dog coat is athletic attire, because dogs are very athletic by nature. However, this sort of dog athletic gear turned out to be rather difficult to find back then.

Things are actually much better today than they were in 2002. Small lapdogs have been popular long enough that it's now relatively easy to find nice fleece jackets for them, both in retail stores and by mail order. Back in 2002, though, the online market seemed to cater mostly to children (and to adults with arrested development) who wanted to "dress up" their little dogs as if they were Barbie dolls.

There were all sorts of costumes available, that I remember finding online back then, lines of extraordinarily impractical designer clothing: Evening dresses, handbags, swimsuits, that sort of thing. Really stuff right out of Barbie's closet. I remember, for example, stumbling upon a website that offered "Jimmy Chew" shoes for little dogs that actually had HIGH HEELS! For goodness sakes, I thought, who buys this stuff? None of it was appropriate as real clothing, to be worn for warmth or for protection from the rain and snow.

The other place to go looking for little dog clothing back then—other than online—was at one of the "big box" pet stores that had sprung up in the nineties, most of which seemed to feature, somewhere in the store, a rack of slightly more practical-looking dog attire. I say "practical-looking" because when you got down to trying these dog clothes on your little dog, they often didn't work out so well. A cute looking "dog parka," for example, often had a large draggy faux-fur trimmed hood that would flop down and interfere with the dog's walking.

I remember standing with Sadie in front of a large and disorganized rack of dog clothes at our local big box pet store, and being very unhappy with the selection. The good thing was that at least they would let you bring your dog into the store to try things on. I held Sadie's leash, hoping that she wouldn't attack the other dogs that came by, while I gazed perplexed at the rack. The few acceptable dog jackets I was able to locate—the ones that weren't too stiff or impractical—all seemed to be sold out in Sadie's potential sizes— Small or Extra-small. There seemed to be plenty of Medium and Large coats that were far too big for my little dog, as well as lots of XX-small and XXX-small sweaters and jackets that were so tiny even little Sadie wouldn't be able to squeeze into them. Who wore these jackets, I wondered. Did they really make dogs that small?

Not being able to find Sadie's correct size, after diligently searching the entire rack, I stood around listlessly for awhile—as one does in such stores—until I could buttonhole a woman wearing a store uniform, who happened to stroll by trying not to meet my eyes.

"Excuse me," I called out to her, "Do you think you might have this in small or extra-small?" I held up one of the more basic-looking dog jackets.

The uniformed woman gazed at the coat for a moment, and then back at me and my dog. You had the feeling that she had been through this "trying on" little dog clothes routine before, and that it hadn't gone well.

"Really anything in small or extra-small would be fine," I said. "We're kind of desperate here."

"Do you want me to look in the back?" the woman said.

"Could you?" I asked. I could see that this person probably did not get paid based upon her level of customer service, or for searching for things in the back for finicky customers like me.

"I'll see what I can find," she said, and ambled off towards the rear of the store.

I had the decided impression that she was headed out back for a smoke, and then planned to return and say, "Nope, couldn't find anything." My faith in humanity was restored, however, when this person came back nearly an hour later (or so it seemed) with a red and green Christmas sweater in size

"Small Dogs Need Clothes"

Extra-Small. "We aren't putting these out yet," she said. "But this is all we have right now. Most of our winter stuff isn't in yet, and everything from the summer is pretty picked over."

I could have hugged her, if she hadn't already slouched away.

It wasn't anywhere near Christmas yet, but the sweater was about the right size, and reasonably stretchy, if a bit scratchy. It took some doing to squeeze Sadie into it, but— Okay, can I just say here how utterly adorable she looked in her little turtleneck?—*Oh. My. God. So cute!!*

Of course, I was having a swoon over tiny dog clothing on my adorable little dog. *And what would my mother think of that?*—Or so said the voice in my head.

It was at this point that I caught a glimpse of my mother in the "changing room" mirror. Yes—the dog clothing rack had a mirror at one end with a sign over it, hand lettered in black marker, that said "changing room" (which someone had apparently written as a joke). Naturally, it wasn't my mother I was seeing in the mirror, but myself.

I'm sure other women have had this experience, of reaching a certain age and then suddenly seeing their mothers in the mirror. In my case, this wasn't necessarily a bad thing. My mother had always been an attractive person with high cheekbones and fluffy auburn hair, and she had remained admirably slender and attractive her whole life. More slender than me, in fact, so this must have been one of those "kind" mirrors that deduct a few pounds, which was why I was suddenly seeing my mother in it. Still, I had a start, seeing her there, trying tiny dog clothes on little Sadie.

I looked at my mother, holding Sadie up in her new red and green Christmas sweater, and had a strange thought. I realized that my mother hadn't lived long enough to be bitten by the tiny lapdog craze. But she was always a stylish person, I remembered now, and she probably would have been as taken with these little dogs as the rest of us. And, if she'd gotten a small dog of her own, she easily could have ended up shopping right here in this same store for small dog clothes, just as I was now doing.

I don't know why it took me so long to realize this. My mother was always a kind-hearted person. She wouldn't have let a tiny dog shiver.

I think that we tend unfairly to freeze our departed loved-ones, and to think of them only as they were, when we knew them. But of course, if my mother had lived long enough, she would not have remained frozen in time, but would have moved forward along with the rest of us.

And she probably would have come to love little Sadie, I thought now. If for no other reason than that she was mine.

I examined Sadie's new sweater, and tugged at it. It fit reasonably well. A little snug, perhaps, but that way it wouldn't sag on our walks if it got wet.

"So what do you think?" I asked my mother, in the mirror. "Shall we take it?"

She nodded her head in approval.

"Let's do it," I said.

My mother smiled.

It wasn't until later on, in December of that year, that I was finally able to get Sadie a really good dog jacket, the one she really needed to survive the long New England winters. I happened to go to a dog show right before Christmas with my friend Melissa, who wanted to look at the Standard

Schnauzers. There were lots of booths at the show selling dog-related merchandise. Melissa, who had previously shopped for coats for her dog Echo, introduced me to a custom dog jacket maker, a wonderful seamstress who had a booth full of samples. The prices were astronomical in my eyes—for a dog coat—but I could send in Sadie's measurements and get back a waterproof, fleece-lined jacket that really fit her—which was what she desperately needed.

I picked out a high quality trench coat for Sadie that I still have somewhere to this day. It was made from a pretty brown raincoat material, and insulated with striped blue fleece, and had broad red decorative straps that closed with Velcro around my dog's belly and chest, holding her securely inside. The coat was well worth the expense, and was really the only one Sadie ever needed, once she grew her fur back. Having a good lined raincoat was the difference between having a shivering, unhappy dog outside, and a dry warm one.

These days, of course, you don't have to go to these lengths to find a nice dog jacket for your little dog. Fleece dog jackets and dog raincoats are now sold everywhere, including often at human retail stores. And there are so many online dog clothes retailers that the cost of even a good custom-made jacket has come way down. There is no longer any reason for a tiny lapdog like Sadie not to be warm, dry and stylish, on even the coldest winter day.

If, that is, you can get over how frivolous it feels to be shopping for tiny little dog clothes.

Chapter 17

NARRATIVE

In the end, my promise to return Sadie to the Piero kids was never really put to the test. Later in the fall we heard, through friends, that Bob Piero was getting remarried to his girlfriend, now fiancé, and that "she didn't like dogs." (So, presumably, the Pieros wouldn't want Sadie or Bandit back.) Not long after this, we also heard that the Pieros were moving away to Florida. Either Bob Piero or his new wife had a job down there. I can't remember exactly what we were told. In any event, it seemed in retrospect like one of those long, bloodless and internecine battles that winds up being won without a shot being fired.

Even that, though, still wasn't quite enough for me. I still couldn't completely let go of my entanglement with Tessa Piero. *Who knew if the rumors we were hearing were true, or not?*— Or so I thought. Maybe those were just things people I knew were telling me, to put my mind at ease.

And so I continued to feel the lingering force of the promises I had made. The Piero kids had disappeared, but nothing ever felt quite resolved. Not until one morning before school, in late November or early December, when

Dan suddenly came to me, his face looking feverish. At first I thought he was coming down with something. I put out my hand to feel his forehead.

"It's been six months," he said.

"What?" I asked. I didn't know what he was talking about.

"Six months, Mom!" he repeated. He dragged me by the hand over to the calendar on the dining room table, and started rattling through the months, counting. "Six," he said at last, putting an insistent finger down firmly on the current month. "Sadie's ours now." He looked at me. "Right?" I could see him scrutinizing my face.

I don't think I had realized until that moment what a burden all of this "back-and-forthing" about Sadie had placed on my young son. It seems to me now, though, that he must have had some sense of the drama that had been going on inside of me.

Of course, Daniel couldn't know everything about my past. I hadn't told him much about losing my father when I was a little older than Tessa, or about losing my mother more recently. But smart, sensitive Dan—he could feel the weight of the struggle within me over this little dog—with that strange sixth sense our children often seem to have about us. He could feel me holding back whenever he asked for assurances about keeping Sadie. Poor Daniel—he was the one person in the world who followed closely everything that I said and did. He could hear me hedging. He knew to hold himself back from loving Sadie too much. She wasn't truly ours yet. Not until this very moment.

"So?" he demanded. "Do we get to keep her? Come ON, Mom."

"Yes," I said quietly, after checking the calendar myself. "She's really ours now."

I shall never forget the sound of Daniel screeching through the house that morning, looking for Sadie and screaming, "Sadie, did you hear that? You're really ours!! You're really ours!!" He found the little dog and hugged her to him, tears streaming down his face, and continued to croon, "You're ours! You're really ours!"

I drove Dan to school that morning, and then it seemed like a little party was in order. I stopped at our local bakery and picked up some muffins for the two dogs and myself. Then I went home and organized a little "Sadie gets to stay party." I didn't have party hats, though I imagine them in my memory. In reality I had to make do with birthday candles shoved into corn muffins.

We sat around one of Daniel's little plastic toy tables from childhood—an item that would be left behind in our move to Hingham. Each of us had a place—me and the two dogs. Willow sat on the floor, waiting patiently to be told that he could eat his corn muffin. Sadie sat in one of the little plastic chairs that went with the table set. I broke her off a piece of Willow's muffin and put some string cheese on it. Then I blew out the candles. "Welcome home, Sadie," I told her.

It really did feel like Sadie was ours now. And soon after this we were finally able to close on the condo, and move away to Hingham, and away from any lingering sense of obligation to the Pieros that I may have felt.

Would we have given Sadie back to the Piero kids, if they had asked within the promised six months? It's hard to say. Steve and Dan certainly would have fought me, but in the end they probably would have left it up to me to decide. I was the one in charge of the household, and the one who walked the dogs every day, and took care of them.

It has taken a long time for me to process everything that happened, and to come to see that a lot of the drama over keeping Sadie was all in my own head. Somewhere along the way I began to understand that everything I had done to "spare the feelings" of the Piero kids had succeeded only in enmeshing me with them further. And the more I thought about it, the more my own motivations seemed suspect. Had I done it all on purpose? Was I a bit too fascinated by what was happening in the Piero household due to my own past losses? Was that why I had taken Sadie in the first place? And over the summer did I allow myself to get sucked into the situation with Tessa visiting for reasons that I barely understood? The answers to all of these questions, as I see it now, were probably "yes." As I have said, I was no saint in rescuing Sadie. And I probably should have cut things off with Tessa much sooner.

Though even that decision—not to do anything at all—I can't help but second-guess. Maybe in the end it was the best thing to let Tessa visit for a time, as the other mothers on the point clearly thought it was. Perhaps that did soften the blow for her, of losing her little dog. It is one of those things that I will never really know.

The thing that I do know is that I felt a great affinity for Tessa, and for what she was going through, losing her mother so young. It's hard to describe what it is like, losing a parent that way—when you are 9, or 10, or 13. Those are such strange ages for anyone, when you are first coming into full human consciousness, out of the obliviousness of childhood.

I remember being 9 or 10 years old, about Tessa's age, and standing outside by myself on a dark winter night on our doorstep outside our house in upstate New York. I was probably calling in the dog, or something like that. But I remember standing out there by myself for a little longer than I needed to—just to feel the boundaries of myself—to feel my growing consciousness against the expanse of white snow and starry black sky. I remember how alone I felt. And how remote and unreachable other human beings seemed. It felt as if I were marooned inside my own body with all of those adolescent feelings coming on.

Imagine now, alongside coming into this sense of isolated and blooming consciousness, the loss of a parent. Our parents are like a warm embracing hug, holding us and comforting us, and keeping us from the harsh universal night until we are old enough to face it ourselves. And when we lose that, when too soon we enter that dark existential space by ourselves—Well, let us just say that I cannot truly describe the abject terror I felt at losing my father at age 13. Of course, I still had my mother. Thank God for that. And Tessa, she still had her father.

Still, it was that same existential terror that I felt moving closer each time Tessa Piero came to visit. I could see it in her eyes, smell the haunt of it on her breath.

When she came for Sadie, it felt to me as if she was coming, not just for her dog, but to retrieve her sense of normalcy that her little dog represented to her. If only she could get Sadie back, then things would return to the way they had been before her mother died. And I—I was standing in the way of that hopeless dream.

We were both running up against a hard truth, Tessa and I—for the terrors of the soul cannot be negotiated,

Narrative

or assuaged. They simply are. It is, in the end, a terrifying thing to be human. To live marooned in our bodies, and then someday to have to face—not just our own mortality—but the deaths of everyone we have ever loved, unless we ourselves go before them.

As adults, we learn ways to cope with this bitter truth— We go to church, develop our own sense of spirituality. Find ways to make it better.

As for children, we can only hope that they are not asked to do this work before they are truly ready, and that we can shelter them a little from the harsh realities of life until they are old enough to deal with them.

I think I felt that summer that Tessa was going through some variation on all of this—but perhaps, again, I am only crediting her with things that were going on inside my own mind. The truth is, I can never really know what Tessa was thinking, those times that she visited.

I do remember one thing, from the last time Tessa and I spoke. It didn't seem significant at the time, but I do remember her saying "thank you" to me on one of the last occasions that she visited. This was a little unusual, I suppose. I rarely got to exchange two words with her. The three young girls usually just raced into the house to get Sadie, found her, and then raced away again with the dog, without giving me the chance to do more than sputter after them, "Have her back by dinner," or something of that ilk.

But on this day, near the end of her series of visits, Tessa did stop long enough to say, "Thank you for doing this." As in, thank you for letting me come and take Sadie out. It seemed an odd thing for a ten year old to stop long enough to say, especially one so bent on ignoring me. I didn't think much of it at the time, but as Tessa ceased coming soon thereafter, this comment later took on more weight in my eyes. There was a certain formality to this statement. It was the sort of thing you said at the end of a visit to someone's house. "Thank you for doing this." So perhaps young Tessa already knew that her new stepmother didn't want to take the dog, or that her family would be moving away to Florida soon. I have no way of knowing.

Still, no matter how often I think of this little scene, it always feels to me as if my mind is trying to invent a narrative, a story that will put a neat ending on things. But that story would, I think, be essentially untruthful.

I can never really know what it all looked like to Tessa Piero, or for that matter to Bob Piero or Robbie Piero. To them, I was probably just some lady down the road who they handed their little dog over to, and that was the end of it. When Tessa visited her friends, and came to take Sadie out for the afternoon, who knows what she really thought?

I considered, once, during the writing of this book, trying to ask her. I wondered what Tessa would remember, or if she would even remember anything at all. I had blocked out a lot of things at her age, after losing my father. Perhaps she would remember exactly nothing. That would, in a way, I thought, be as interesting as if she remembered things differently from the way I had.

I went online and searched for girls by her name who lived in Florida. She would, I calculated, just be starting college at the time I did my search. And I did actually find a record of a girl by her name who had graduated recently from a Florida high school. I was pretty sure it was Tessa.

Narrative

This girl had the same angular face and dark hair. Part of her yearbook was online, and there was a picture of her huddled with one or two friends, just the way I remembered her huddling with her friends on our point.

I think it was good that I went through this exercise of searching for Tessa, because it quickly put into focus for me that she had probably had her own drama, her own narrative about what happened that summer, and that the story told in this book wasn't really about her at all. It was about me, and what I'd gone through, and about coming to grips with losing my parents. If Tessa did remember anything, I realized, it would be bound up in her own narrative, one about losing her mother Calista, and it was likely to convey a very different story than the one I have told here.

That is the nature of narrative, finally, I realized. To carry the stories of our lives, and to make sense of what we have been through—hopefully in a way that helps us to remember and that puts things into perspective.

It would be presumptuous, I realized, for me to try and sum up Tessa's story for her. Perhaps she will write her own story one of these days.

Chapter 18

CLAIRVOYANCE

The world has changed dramatically since 2002. Where once tiny lapdogs had seemed a harbinger of the housing boom, and appropriate only for starlets and young girls, they now seem emblematic of an effort on the part of many Americans to downsize in response to forces like the financial crash, the housing crisis, and global warming. A new austerity has set in.

There seems to be a whole new generation coming along, of young people who appear to feel more comfortable renting apartments in the city and taking mass transit, rather than moving to the suburbs and driving cars. They seem to fear becoming over-extended financially, with mortgages and student loans, and the like. They are especially leery of being anchored by home ownership when they may need to be able to relocate quickly in order to pursue the diminishing number of available jobs in an increasingly global marketplace.

Small dogs seem to suit this newly mobile and urbanized lifestyle. Little dogs are also a good fit for a large contingent of "empty nester" boomers, who themselves are increasingly downsizing from houses as they approach retirement, and take up residence in apartments or condos, or over-55 communities. Cars, too, are shrinking with the rising cost of fuel and a warming planet. Somehow, larger dogs seem more and more impractical for a lot of people these days.

It remains to be seen whether these trends will continue as the economy improves, or whether full employment will return, and breathe new life and affluence back into the American suburbs. Perhaps large mansions, and big cars and big dogs, will again become popular. Or perhaps the grinding forces of globalization and digitization will permanently reshape the American landscape, as such technological changes have done in the past.

The one thing that seems clear is this: The little dogs are here to stay. I sincerely doubt that those of us who have become acquainted with these little lapdogs will ever want to completely give up on these smallest of our domesticated wolves.

There are, I suppose, still a few final grace notes to add, in ending this story, about life with a rescued lapdog. Although Sadie now felt utterly and totally like ours, and would live a long and happy life with us—in some ways she was never completely ours. She had had at least two other "lives" before coming to live with us—her life as a puppy mill dog and her life with the Piero family. And those experiences had left a permanent mark upon her that she would never entirely lose.

We never did completely solve the problem of Sadie attacking other dogs, for example—this despite long and assiduous training. And I came to believe—as I have said— that this was due to her lack of socialization as a puppy mill puppy. Sadie did eventually meet a dog who was "not amused" by being attacked. Fortunately, this dog was not a huge dog that snapped Sadie in two, but rather was a small Welsh terrier, named Thelma, whom we met a couple of years later at our local dog park in Hingham.

Thelma was adorable—she looked like a tiny perfect Airedale—and I had taken to slipping her dog treats when I saw her in the park. One day, though, when I was out in the park with Sadie and Willow, Thelma came by to say hello (and get her cookie), and Sadie decided to light into her for some reason.

Thelma was a terrier. Terriers, I will tell you right now, do not take kindly to being attacked, particularly when the attack is unprovoked, and when there is a cookie involved.

Thelma whirled about upon Sadie, threw her over on her back, and stood over her growling harshly at her with her big white terrier choppers inches from Sadie's jugular vein. Sadie lay there on her back, screaming her head off—in a high-pitched "I'm being killed" sort of scream.

Thelma did not actually bite Sadie, and her owner quickly called her off—but Sadie was shaken for days. Thelma had made it clear that she meant to rip Sadie's lungs out through her throat. The encounter between the two dogs had not been a pretty one.

Following this incident, Sadie's attitude about other dogs seemed noticeably to change. She would still growl at other dogs when she saw them in the park, but instead of attacking, she would go and hide behind a tree. Or, if there was no tree, behind me or another person. She seemed finally to understand that she was putting herself in danger by attacking other dogs, and, in hiding, it was almost as if she were hiding from her own worst impulses.

Clairvoyance

After the "Thelma incident," the only dogs Sadie would still attack were Golden Retrievers. Why Goldens? I wondered. I remembered that her old housemate Bandit was a Golden, but Sadie had gotten along fine with him. In fact, she had dominated the poor beast. Perhaps she was still trying to dominate Goldens? Or perhaps she'd had a bad experience with another Golden?

Really, it was impossible to know. But that is something you come to realize when you've had a rescued dog for awhile. They have a whole mysterious past that you will never know anything about.

It is very perplexing, this mysterious past. Strange behaviors often erupt out of nowhere, and you don't really know what to make of them. I have talked with owners of other rescued dogs about this, and they all seem to have stories of this kind—about their dog alerting to strange cars driving by, or growling at certain kinds of people. Or being scared of certain types of places.

In our case, Sadie never completely forgot about the Pieros. Bear with me for one final story, to illustrate.

I kept doing dog training with Sadie, and a year or two later we were enrolled in a small-dog agility class with Bill Sellers. Sadie was still not the world's most obedient or well-behaved dog, but she was doing well enough at agility training for Bill to invite us to participate in an agility demonstration that his dog training club was putting on at a local Pet Expo.

Several members of our class were going to participate in this demonstration (including the fleet of Poms), and Bill had a ring set up at the Pet Expo with agility equipment arranged in a short course especially for smaller dogs. There was, as I recall, an A-frame to climb, and a teeter, and several jumps, and a long tunnel to shoot through. We did a few practice runs on the course with our dogs, and then a small crowd gathered to watch the demonstration.

We were supposed to go around the course two or three times, because it was such a short course. When it was our turn, Sadie and I zipped around the course the first time with no trouble—A-frame, jump, tunnel, jump, jump, teeter—something like that. We were doing reasonably well, so I decided to chance a second trip around the course, even though Sadie was still fairly new to agility competitions.

However, on our second pass around the course, Sadie did the A-frame and the first jump, but then ran behind the tunnel and dashed out through an opening in the ring enclosure, and into the crowd—where she found a couple of ten year old girls standing, one of whom bore a striking resemblance to Tessa Piero. The girls were lovely about bringing Sadie back to me, and delivered her wriggling into my arms, much to the amusement of the crowd.

Afterwards, I was a bit amazed by what Sadie had done. How had she—while running an agility course she had never seen before, something she was still fairly new at—had the time to scan a large crowd for ten year old girls, recognize one she thought might be Tessa, then form a plan in her pea-sized brain to leave the agility ring, and go join her?

It is a little boggling to think about, and gives us some sense of how amazing dogs are at looking for and finding old pack members. Sometimes, as with Sadie, we can know who they are looking for. But at other moments, these behaviors make our rescued dogs seem a little more wild, a little more instinctive. Their senses are so much keener than ours, and their pack sensibility so much more developed. At times their practiced ability to scan for old friends can seem almost like a kind of clairvoyance.

And even if they are wrong, as Sadie was that day—the girl was not, after all, Tessa Piero—it still seems that a rescued dog will always be searching, yearning, looking for those whom they have lost.

As their new adoptive families, we can give these dogs love, and try to do our best to care for them, and provide good new homes, but the truth is we can never completely repair the holes left in their hearts when they were ripped from their original kinships. This is perhaps something we can all relate to—we who have lost loved ones.

I would always feel that about Sadie—that the strong desire was always in her to restore her original pack-family. As much as she grew to love us and to depend upon us—on Steve and Dan and me—I don't think she ever completely stopped searching and listening for a certain young girl—one with a familiar angular face and pale blue-green eyes.

END

ABOUT THE AUTHOR

Kimberly Davis is an award-winning poet, and the author of the memoir *Teaching the Dog to Think* and the poetry chapbook *Alchemies of Loss*. She also writes *Kim's Craft Blog*, http://kimscraftblog.blogspot.com, a blog about creative writing craft and the writing life. Davis was the winner of the 2009-2010 James Wright Poetry Award. She currently lives in Hingham, Massachusetts, with her husband, Steve Rider, and son Daniel. For more information about author Kimberly Davis, visit her website at http://kimberlysdavis.com/.

www.ingramcontent.com/pod-product-compliance
Lightning Source LLC
LaVergne TN
LVHW040116080426
835507LV00039B/391